W9-BNQ-880

IN THE FOOTSTEPS OF THE MASTER

PHOTOGRAPHY BY RUSS BUSBY

In the beginning was the Word, and the Word was with God, and the Word was God. And the Word was made flesh, and dwelt among us, (and we beheld his glory, the glory as of the only begotten of the Father,) full of grace and truth.

JOHN 1: 1, 14

IDEALS PUBLISHING CORPORATION
NASHVILLE, TENNESSEE

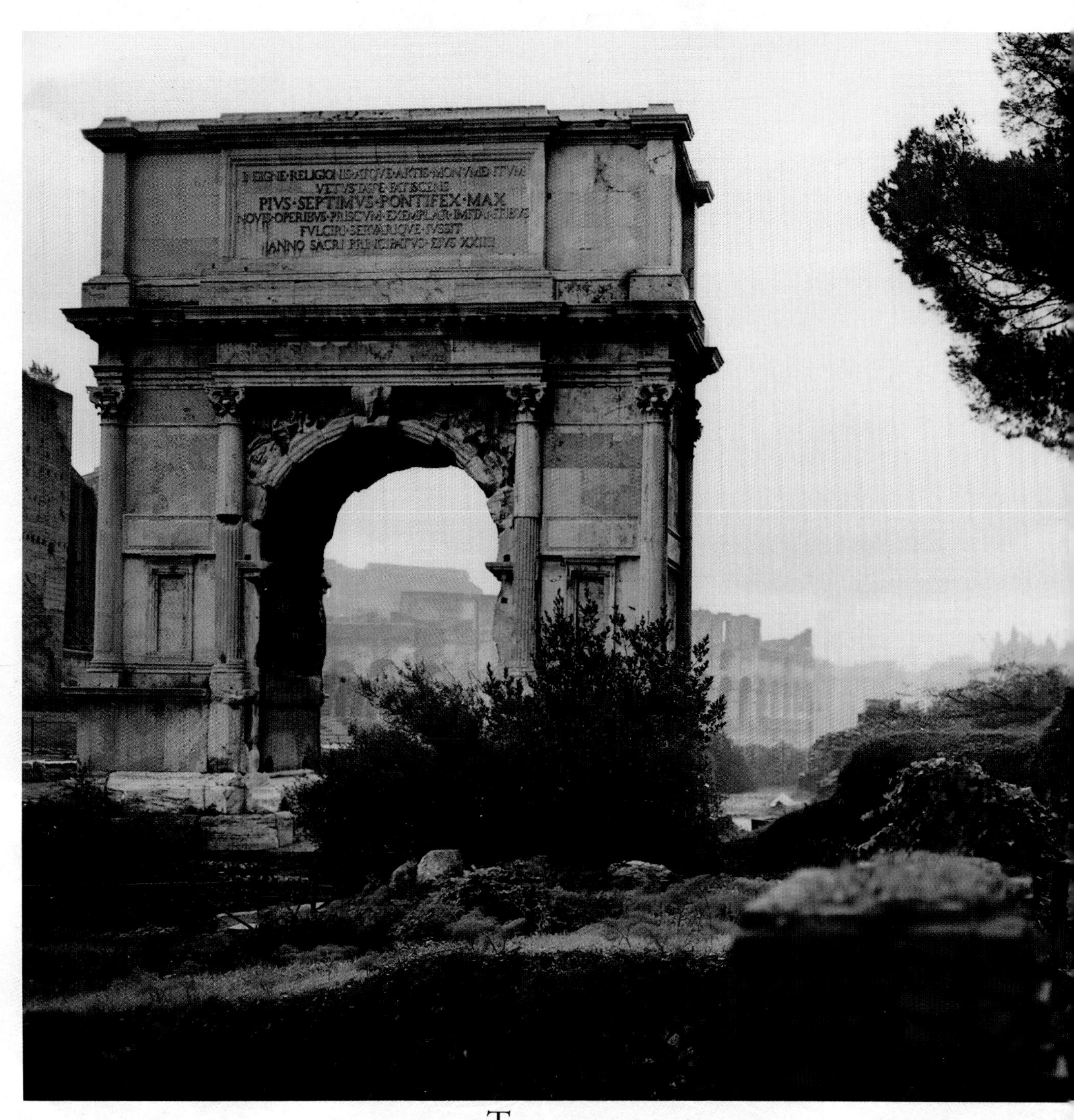

THE ARCH OF TITUS was built in Rome to commemorate Roman victory in the Jewish revolt in Jerusalem in A.D. 70. In taking Jerusalem, the Emperor Titus destroyed the temple of Herod the Great, fulfilling Jesus' prophecy that "there shall not be left here one stone upon another, that shall not be thrown down."

CONTENTS

Text copy set in Adobe Garamond, Italic; Photo captions and display type set in Adobe Garamond
Type composed by Goeser & Goeser; Large initial capital letters designed and hand-lettered by Patrick McRae

Publisher, Patricia A. Pingry; Editor, Nancy J. Skarmeas; Associate Editor, D. Fran Morley; Book Designer, Patrick McRae
Color separations by Rayson Films, Waukesha, Wisconsin; Printed and bound by Ringier America, Brookfield, Wisconsin

All rights reserved. No part of this publication may be reproduced or transmitted in any form or by any means, electronic or mechanical, including photocopy, recording, or any information storage and retrieval system, without permission in writing from the publisher.

Copyright © 1991 by Ideals Publishing Corporation, Nashville, Tennessee

Bible quotations from The King James Version of the Holy Bible

ISBN 0-8249-4043-1

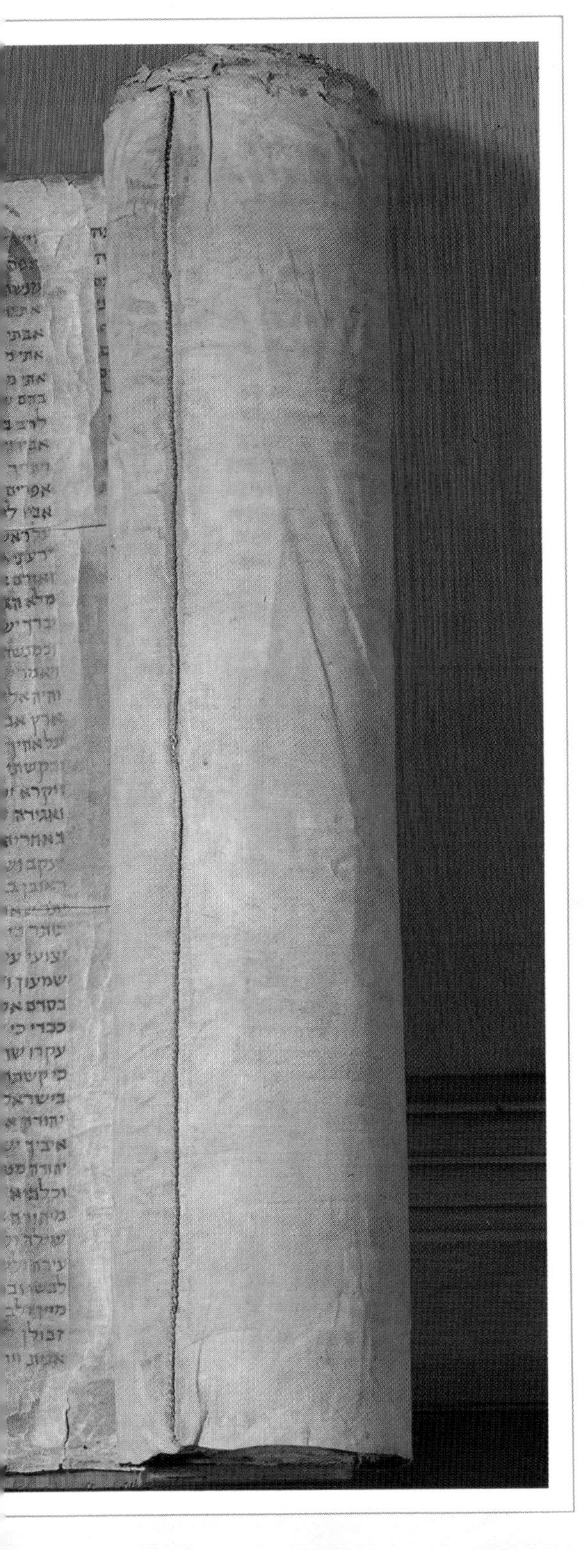

THE PROPHECY

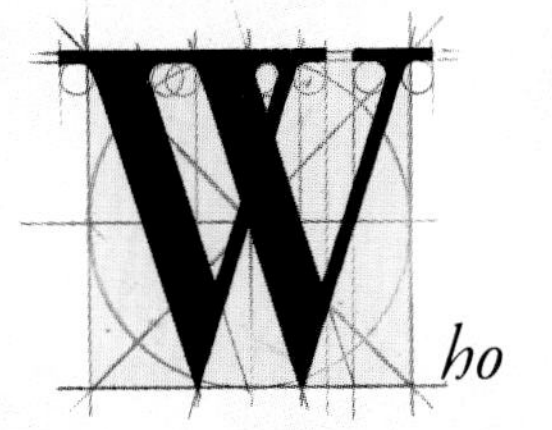*ho*

hath believed our report?

and to whom is the arm

of the Lord revealed?

ISAIAH 53: 1

THE PENTATEUCH, from the Greek *Pentateukhos,* meaning five scrolls, is the first five books of the Bible; to the Jews, it is the Book of Law or the Torah. The Pentateuch pictured dates from the fifteenth century.

Biblical scholars believe the STAR OF BETHLEHEM was a super nova, an exploding star, or a rare alignment of planets. The Wise Men who followed the star were of a priestly caste of the Medes in Persia and would have noticed any unfamiliar object in the night sky.

or unto us a child is born, unto us a son is given: and the government shall be upon his shoulder: and his name shall be called Wonderful, Counsellor, The mighty God, The everlasting Father, The Prince of Peace.

Of the increase of his government and peace there shall be no end, upon the throne of David, and upon his kingdom, to order it, and to establish it with judgment and with justice from henceforth even for ever. The zeal of the Lord of hosts will perform this.

ISAIAH 9: 6, 7

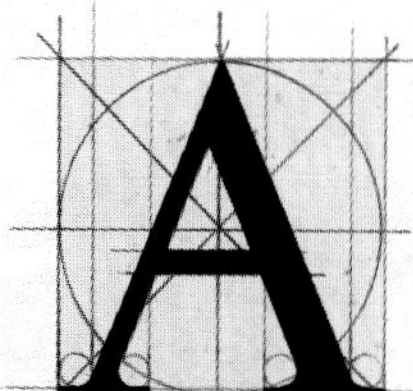

nd there
shall come forth a rod out of the stem of Jesse,
and a Branch shall grow out of his roots:
And the spirit of the Lord
shall rest upon him,
the spirit of wisdom and understanding,
the spirit of counsel and might,
the spirit of knowledge
and of the fear of the Lord;

And shall make him of quick
understanding in the fear of the Lord. . . .
And righteousness shall be
the girdle of his loins,
and faithfulness
the girdle of his reins.
The wolf also shall dwell with the lamb,
and the leopard shall lie down with the kid;
and the calf and the young lion
and the fatling together;
and a little child shall lead them.

ISAIAH 11: 1-3, 5, 6

JERUSALEM, seen here from the Mount of Olives, remains a holy city to Christian, Jew, and Moslem. The golden dome near the center of the photo is the Islamic Dome of the Rock, which stands on ground that was once the site of the Temple of Solomon and later of the temple built under Herod the Great. Under the Dome lies the rock where Abraham prepared to sacrifice Isaac and where all subsequent temple sacrifices were made.

BETHLEHEM, as viewed from the tower of the Church of the Nativity, has changed little since the time of Christ. The ancestral home of King David, Bethlehem is located about five miles south of Jerusalem on an old trade route.

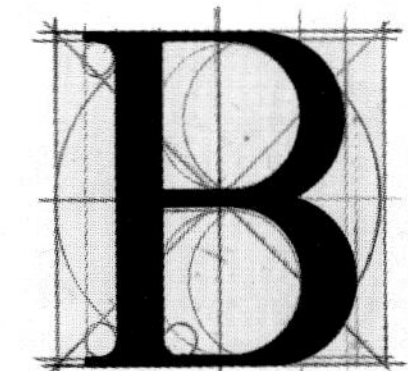

ut thou,
Bethlehem Ephratah, though thou be
little among the thousands of Judah,
yet out of thee shall he come forth
unto me that is to be ruler in Israel;
whose goings forth
have been from of old,
from everlasting.

Then shall we know,
if we follow on to know the Lord:
his going forth is prepared
as the morning;
and he shall come unto us as the rain,
as the latter and former rain
unto the earth.

MICAH 5: 2, HOSEA 6: 3

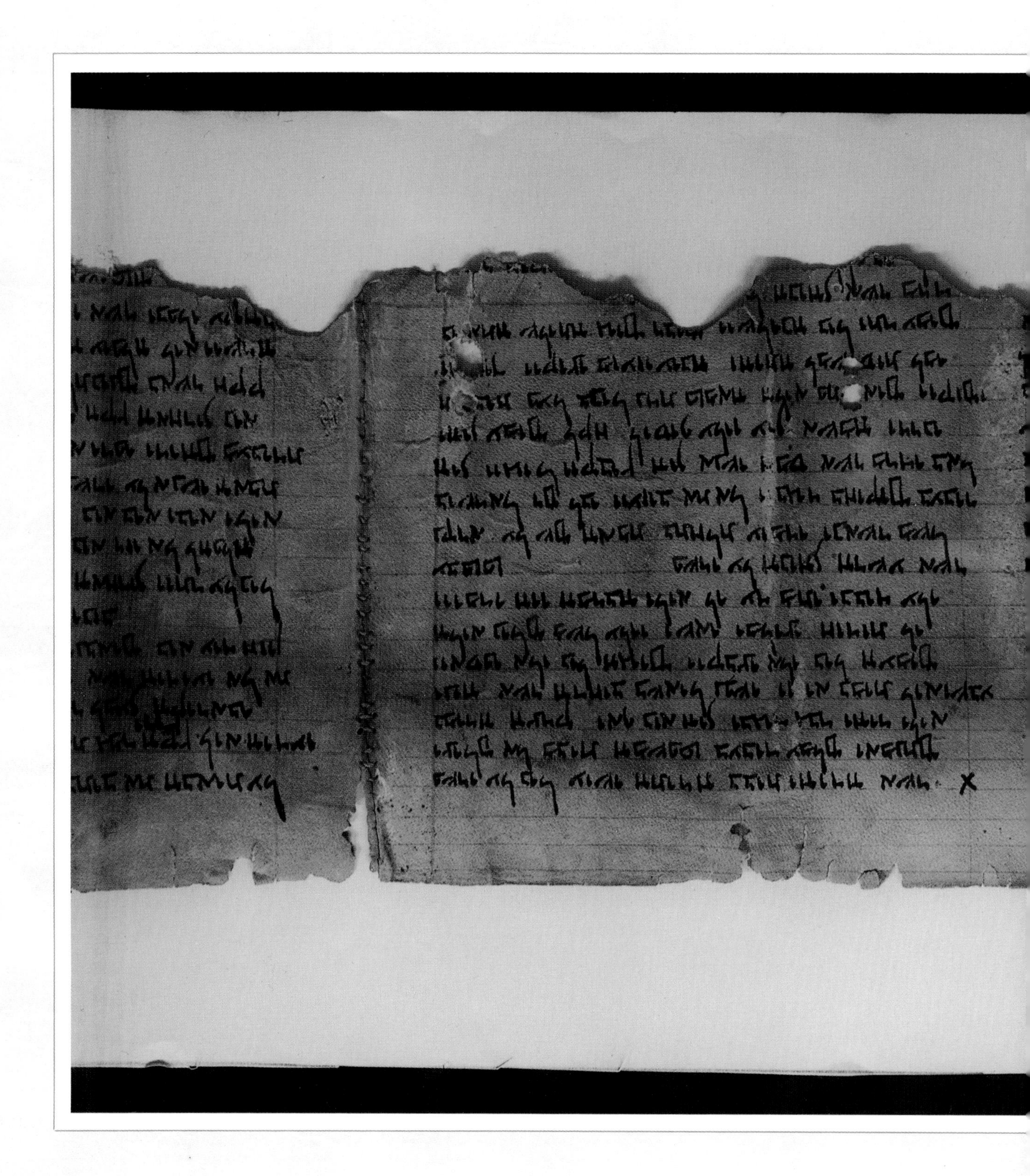

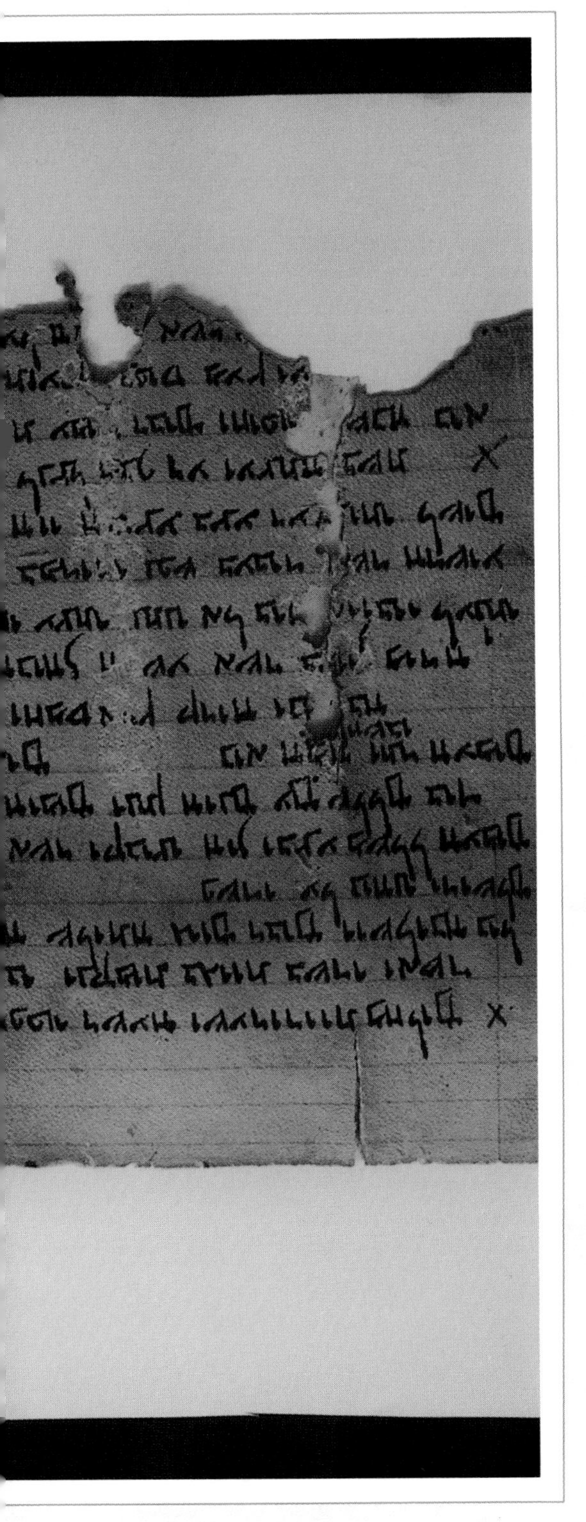

THE EARLY LIFE OF JESUS

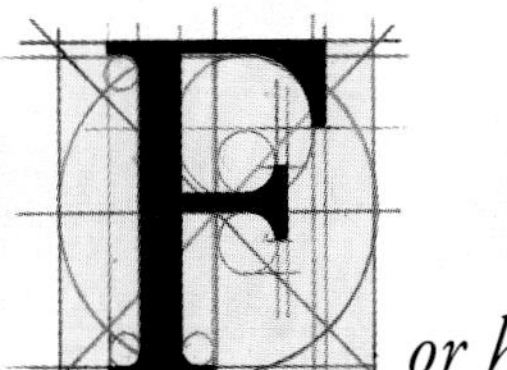

For he shall
grow up before him as a tender plant,
and as a root out of dry ground:
he hath no form nor comeliness;
and when we shall see him,
there is no beauty that we should desire him.

ISAIAH 53: 2

One of the most important Biblical finds in recent history is the discovery of the DEAD SEA SCROLLS (the popular name for approximately 500 scrolls and fragments of scrolls made of vellum—treated sheepskins stitched together). In 1947 the scrolls were found in a cave by a Bedouin shepherd searching for a lost sheep. Scholars believe the scrolls were written between 250 B.C. and A.D. 68. Pictured is a portion of the scrolls, the commentary of the Book of Habakkuk.

NAZARETH, in the Lebanon Mountain range of southern Galilee, lies close to an ancient major trade route but is isolated by steep hills. Because of its seclusion, Nazareth was never a commercially important town and is not mentioned in the Old Testament. It is well known today only because it was the childhood home of Christ.

And in the sixth
month the angel Gabriel was sent from God
unto a city of Galilee, named Nazareth,
To a virgin espoused to a man
whose name was Joseph,
of the house of David;
and the virgin's name was Mary.
And the angel came in unto her, and said,
Hail, thou that art highly favoured,
the Lord is with thee:
blessed art thou among women.
And behold, thou shalt conceive . . . and
bring forth a son, and shalt call his name
JESUS.

He shall be great, and shall be called
the Son of the Highest:
and the Lord God shall give unto him
the throne of his father David:
And he shall reign over the house of Jacob
for ever; and of his kingdom
there shall be no end.

LUKE 1: 26-28, 31-33

*And it came to pass in those days, that there went out a decree from Caesar Augustus, that all the world should be taxed.
And all went to be taxed. . . .*

*And Joseph also went up from Galilee, out of the city of Nazareth, into Judaea, unto the city of David, which is called Bethlehem; (because he was of the house and lineage of David:)
To be taxed with Mary his espoused wife, being great with child.*

*And so it was, that, while they were there, the days were accomplished that she should be delivered.
And she brought forth her firstborn son, and wrapped him in swaddling clothes, and laid him in a manger; because there was no room for them in the inn.*

LUKE 2: 1, 3-7

A CARAVAN, much like that of Mary and Joseph, on the road from Nazareth to Bethlehem. The trip would not have been easy as the road winds over sixty miles of hills, plains, and deserts.

SHEPHERDS GRAZE THEIR SHEEP on the hillsides overlooking Bethlehem as they did in Biblical times. Immediately east of Bethlehem the land is wilderness across the fourteen miles to the Dead Sea.

And there were in the same country shepherds abiding in the field, keeping watch over their flock by night. And, lo, the angel of the Lord came upon them, and the glory of the Lord shone round about them: and they were sore afraid. And the angel said unto them, Fear not: for, behold, I bring you good tidings of great joy, which shall be to all people. For unto you is born this day in the city of David a Saviour, which is Christ the Lord. And this shall be a sign unto you; Ye shall find the babe wrapped in swaddling clothes, lying in a manger.

And suddenly there was with the angel a multitude of the heavenly host praising God, and saying, Glory to God in the highest, and on earth peace, good will toward men.

LUKE 2: 8-14

And it came to pass, as the angels were gone away from them into heaven, the shepherds said one to another, Let us now go even unto Bethlehem, and see this thing which is come to pass, which the Lord hath made known unto us.

And they came with haste, and found Mary, and Joseph, and the babe lying in a manger. And when they had seen it, they made known abroad the saying which was told them concerning this child. And all they that heard it wondered at those things which were told them by the shepherds.

And the shepherds returned, glorifying and praising God for all the things that they had heard and seen, as it was told unto them.

LUKE 2: 15-18, 20

The village of BETHLEHEM was well known in Old Testament times as the home of King David. Because Joseph was a descendant of David, and Mary was his wife, Jesus' birth fulfilled the ancient prophecy that David's kingdom would have no end.

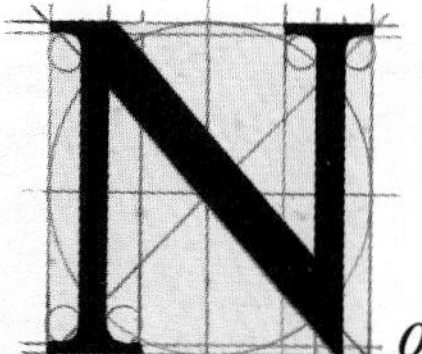

ow when
Jesus was born in Bethlehem of Judaea
in the days of Herod the king,
behold, there came wise men from the east
to Jerusalem, Saying, Where is he
that is born King of the Jews?
for we have seen his star in the east,
and are come to worship him.

When Herod the king had heard these things,
he was troubled,
and all Jerusalem with him.
And when he had gathered all the
chief priests and scribes of the people together,
he demanded of them where
Christ should be born.
And they said unto him,
In Bethlehem of Judaea:
for thus it is written by the prophet. . . .

MATTHEW 2: 1-5

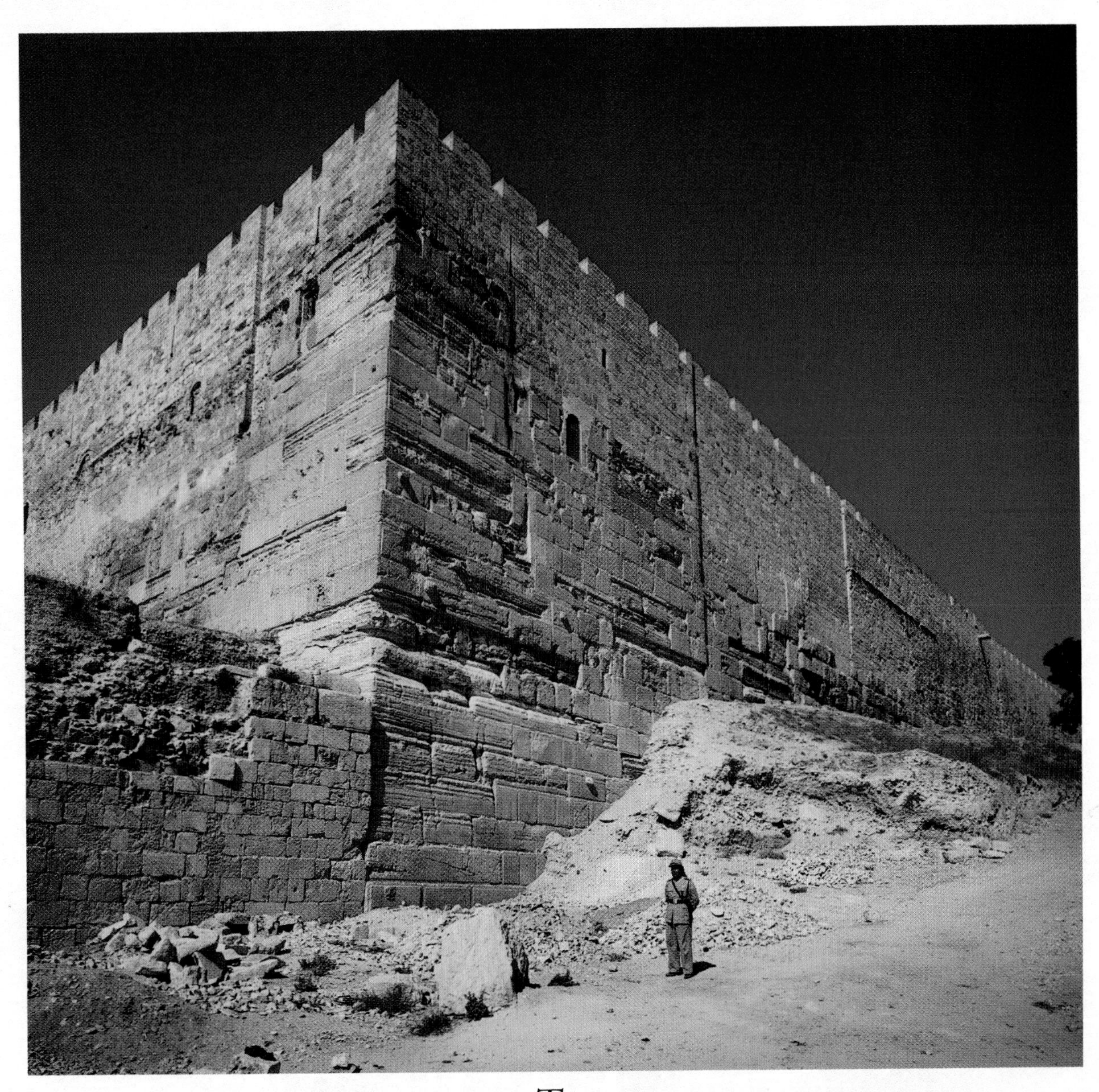

The foundation of the wall of the old city of Jerusalem has recently been unearthed by archaeologists. THE LARGE BLOCKS at the bottom were part of the temple built by Herod the Great and destroyed (as Christ predicted) by the Romans in A.D. 70.

*Behold, the
angel of the Lord appeareth to Joseph
in a dream, saying,
Arise, and take the young child
and his mother, and flee into Egypt,
and be thou there until I bring thee word:
for Herod will seek the young child
to destroy him.*

*When he arose, he took the young child
and his mother by night,
and departed into Egypt:
And was there until the death of Herod:
that it might be fulfilled
which was spoken of the Lord
by the prophet, saying,
Out of Egypt have I called my son.*

MATTHEW 2: 13-15

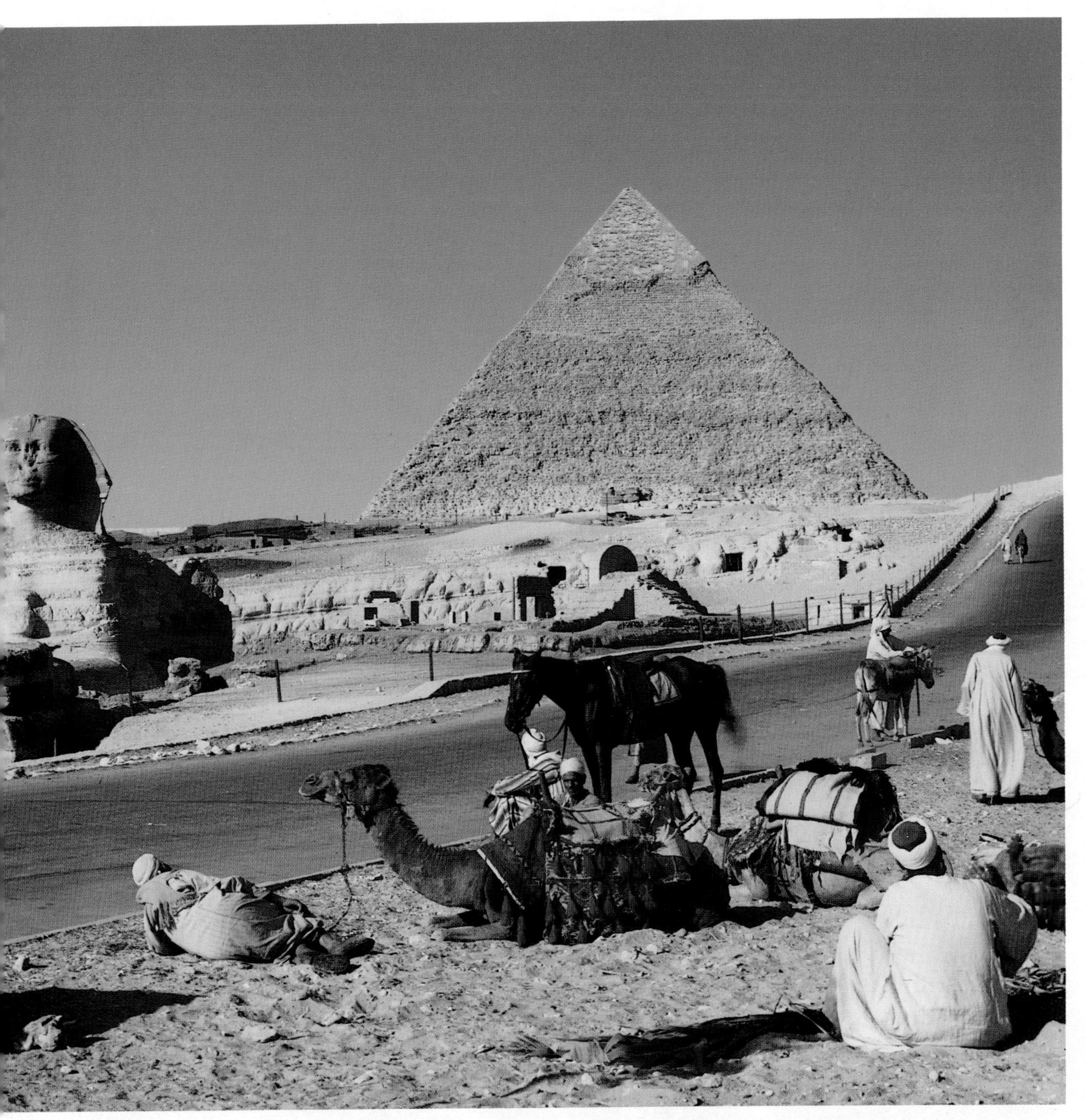

At the time of the Hebrew Exodus, some thirteen hundred years before the birth of Christ, the GREAT PYRAMIDS and the SPHINX at Giza in Egypt were already over one thousand years old.

Then cometh
Jesus from Galilee to Jordan unto John, to be
baptized of him. But John forbad him, saying,
I have need to be baptized of thee,
and comest thou to me?
And Jesus answering said unto him,
Suffer it to be so now: for thus it becometh
us to fulfill all righteousness.
Then he suffered him.

And Jesus, when he was baptized,
went up straightway out of the water:
and, lo, the heavens were opened
unto him, and he saw
the Spirit of God descending like a dove,
and lighting upon him:

And lo a voice from heaven, saying,
This is my beloved Son,
in whom I am well pleased.

MATTHEW 3: 13-17

From its headwaters at the foot of Mount Hermon in present-day Syria, the JORDAN RIVER winds through the desert into the Sea of Galilee. It then continues through the Jordan Valley until it finally empties into the Dead Sea, thirteen hundred feet below sea level. The exact site of Jesus' baptism is not known, but some scholars believe it was just north of the Dead Sea.

This barren DESERT in present-day Jordan is typical of wilderness sites in the region. The tents belong to Bedouin herdsmen, whose way of life has changed very little over the centuries.

*Then was
Jesus led up of the spirit into the wilderness
to be tempted of the devil.
And when he had fasted forty days
and forty nights,
he was afterward an hungred.*

*And when the tempter came to him,
he said, If thou be the Son of God,
command that these stones
be made bread.
But he answered and said,
It is written, Man shall not live
by bread alone,
but by every word that proceedeth
out of the mouth of God.*

MATTHEW 4: 1-4

Then the devil
taketh him up into the holy city, and setteth
him on a pinnacle of the temple,
And saith unto him, If thou be
the Son of God, cast thyself down:
for it is written,
He shall give his angels charge
concerning thee:
and in their hands
they shall bear thee up,
lest at any time
thou dash thy foot against a stone.

Jesus said unto him, It is written
again, Thou shalt not tempt
the Lord thy God.

MATTHEW 4: 5-7

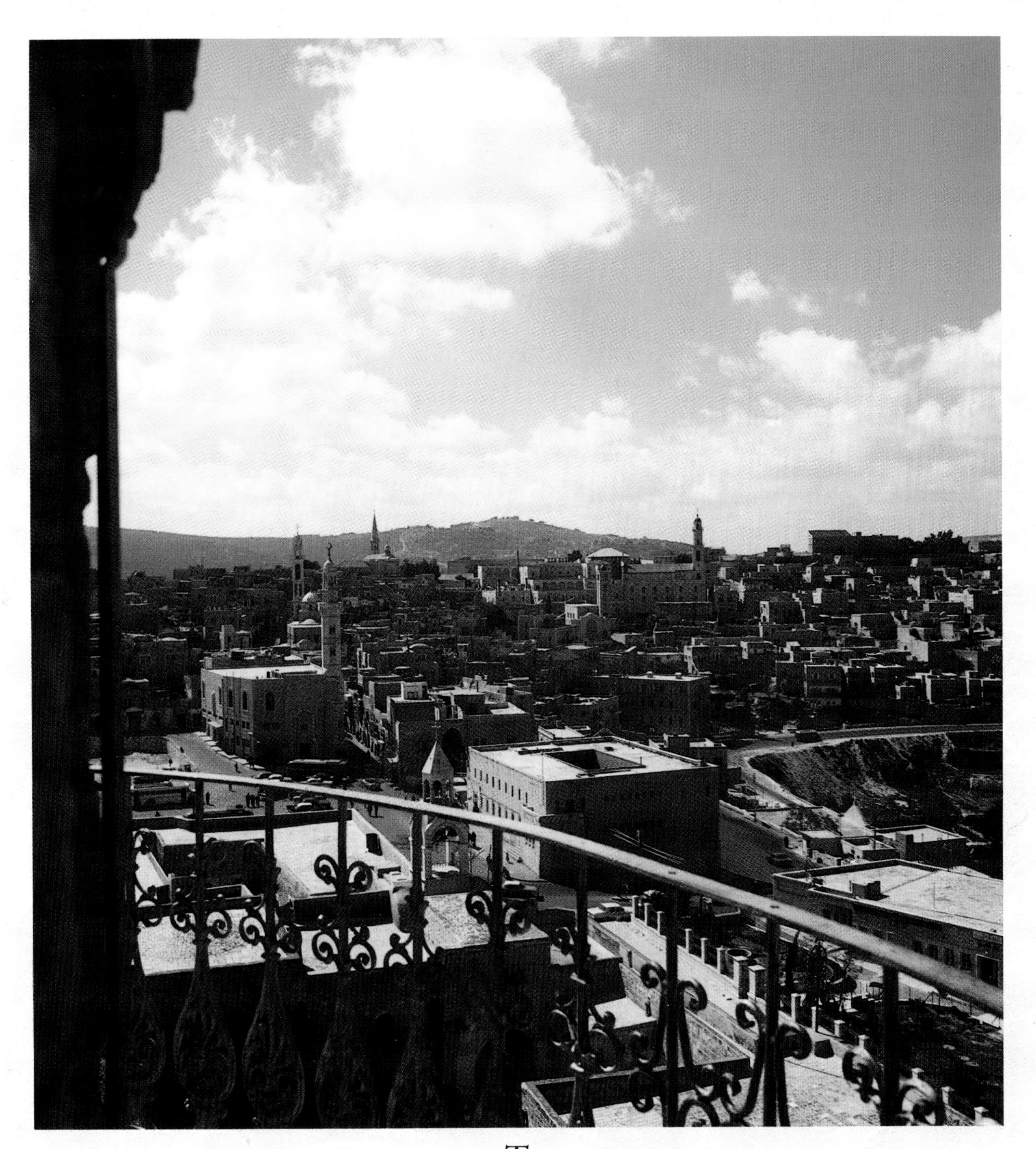

The town of BETHLEHEM was an important stop on the road between Jerusalem and Hebron, the ancestral home of Abraham. Bethlehem is seen here from the Bell Tower of the Church of the Nativity, which was built by the Emperor Constantine in A.D. 325 on the supposed site of Christ's birth.

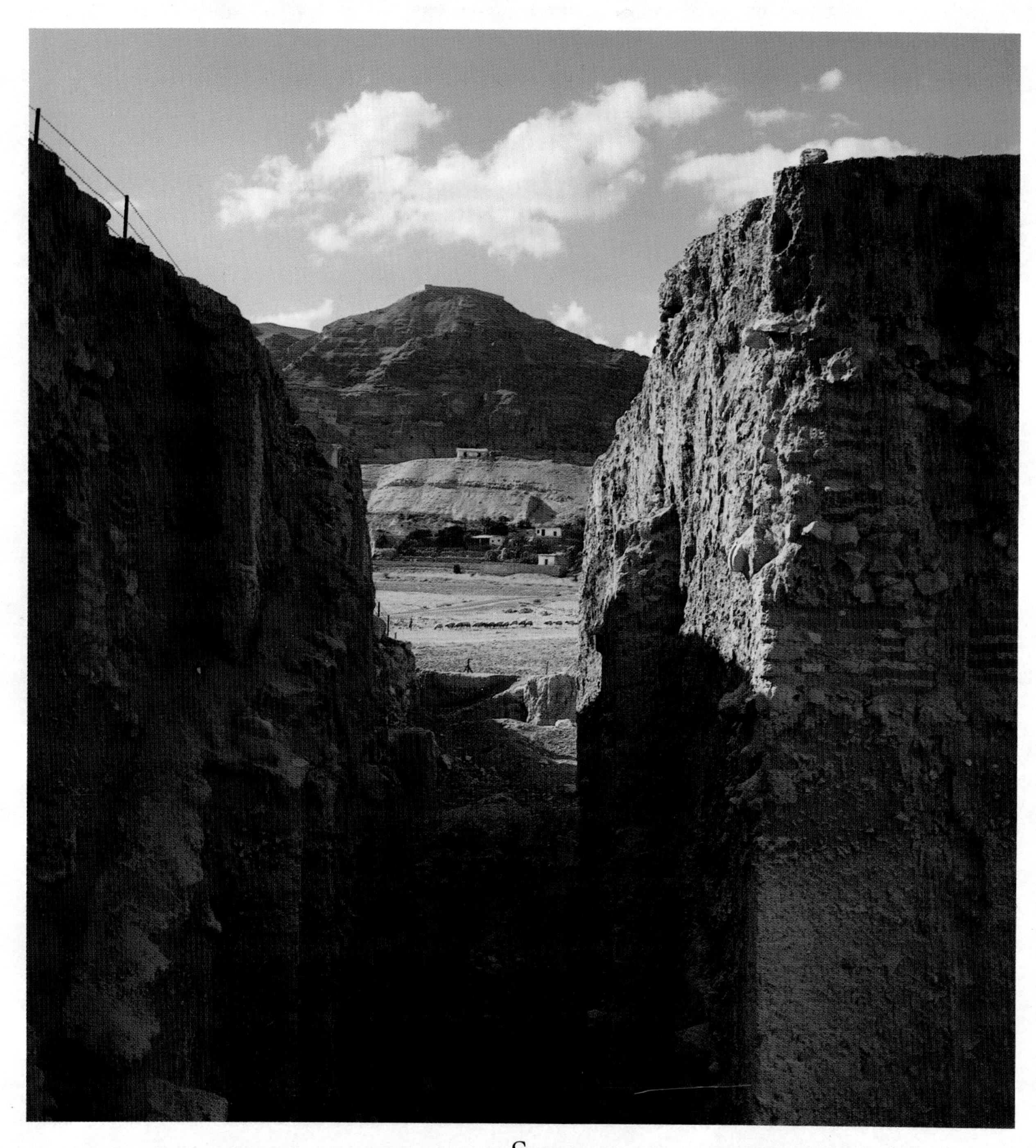

Seen here through the ruins of Jericho, THE MOUNT OF TEMPTATION is also known as *Jebel-Quarantal* (the name means "forty") because of the number of days Jesus fasted. Jericho, one of the oldest inhabited cities in the world, was a favorite city of Herod the Great, who beautified it and is believed to have died there.

Again, the devil taketh him up into an exceeding high mountain, and sheweth him all the kingdoms of the world, and the glory of them;
And saith unto him,
All these things will I give thee,
if thou wilt fall down and worship me.

Then saith Jesus unto him,
Get thee hence, Satan: for it is written,
Thou shalt worship the Lord thy God,
and him only shalt thou serve.
Then the devil leaveth him,
and, behold, angels came
and ministered unto him.

MATTHEW 4: 8-11

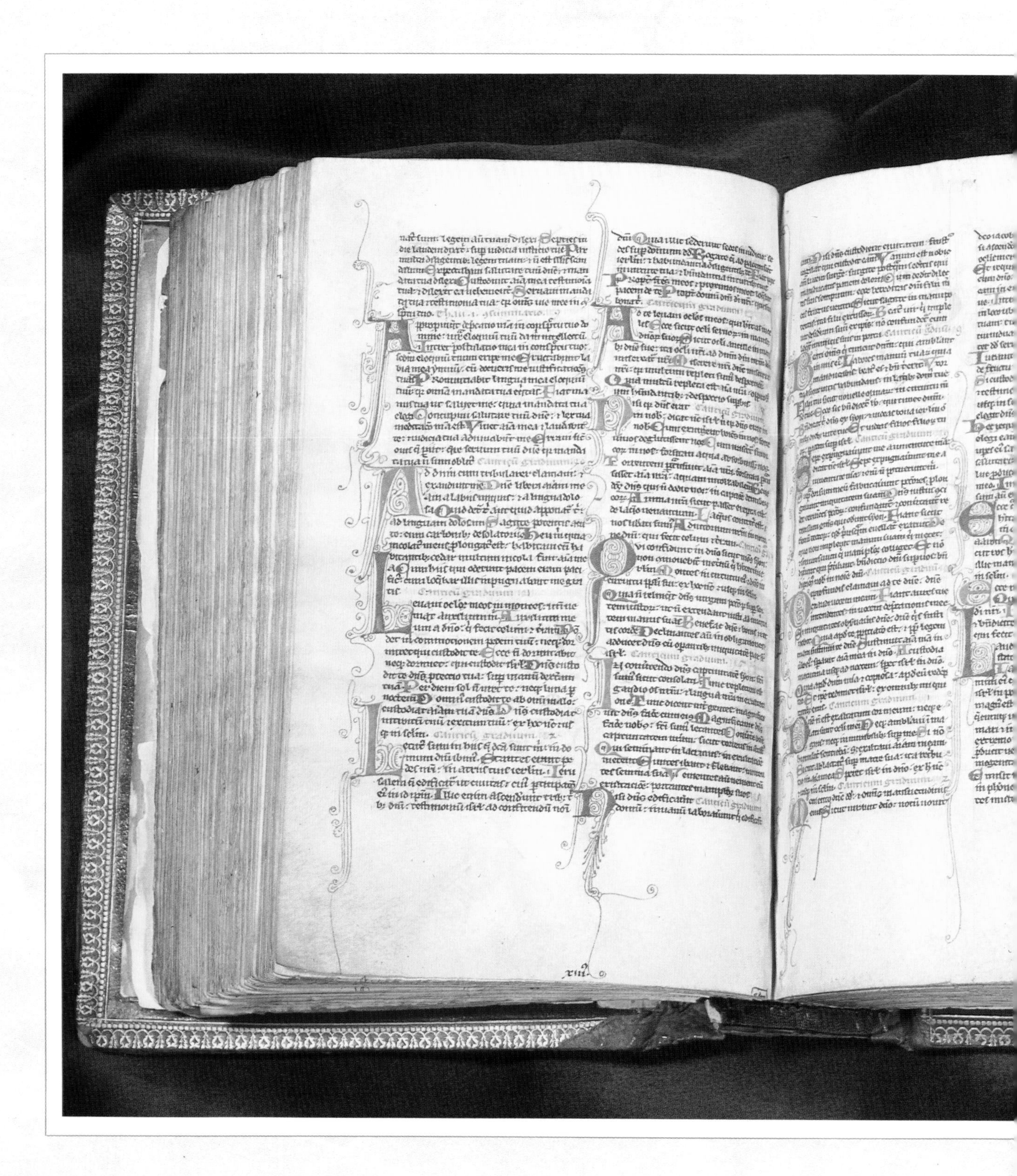

THE MINISTRY

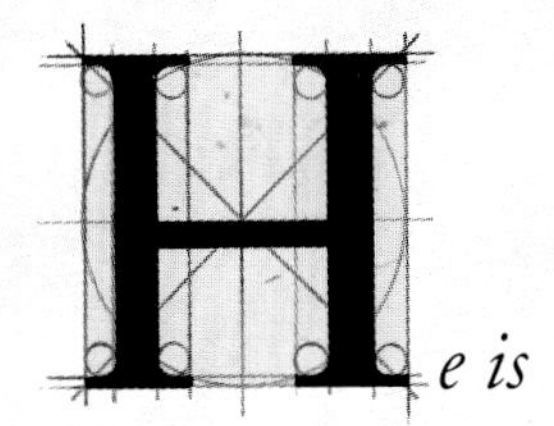

e is

despised and rejected of men;

a man of sorrows,

and acquainted with grief:

and we hid as it were our faces

from him; he was despised,

and we esteemed him not.

ISAIAH 53: 3

In the fifth century, Damasus, the Bishop of Rome, ordered a new Latin translation of the Bible. Earlier versions were translations of translations—from Hebrew to Greek to Latin—but this version, which came to be known as the LATIN VULGATE, was translated directly from the original Hebrew and completed in A.D. 405. The best surviving manuscript of the Latin Vulgate is the *Codex Amiatinus*, presented to Pope Gregory in A.D. 716 and now in the Laurentine Library in Florence, Italy. The copy pictured dates from 1250.

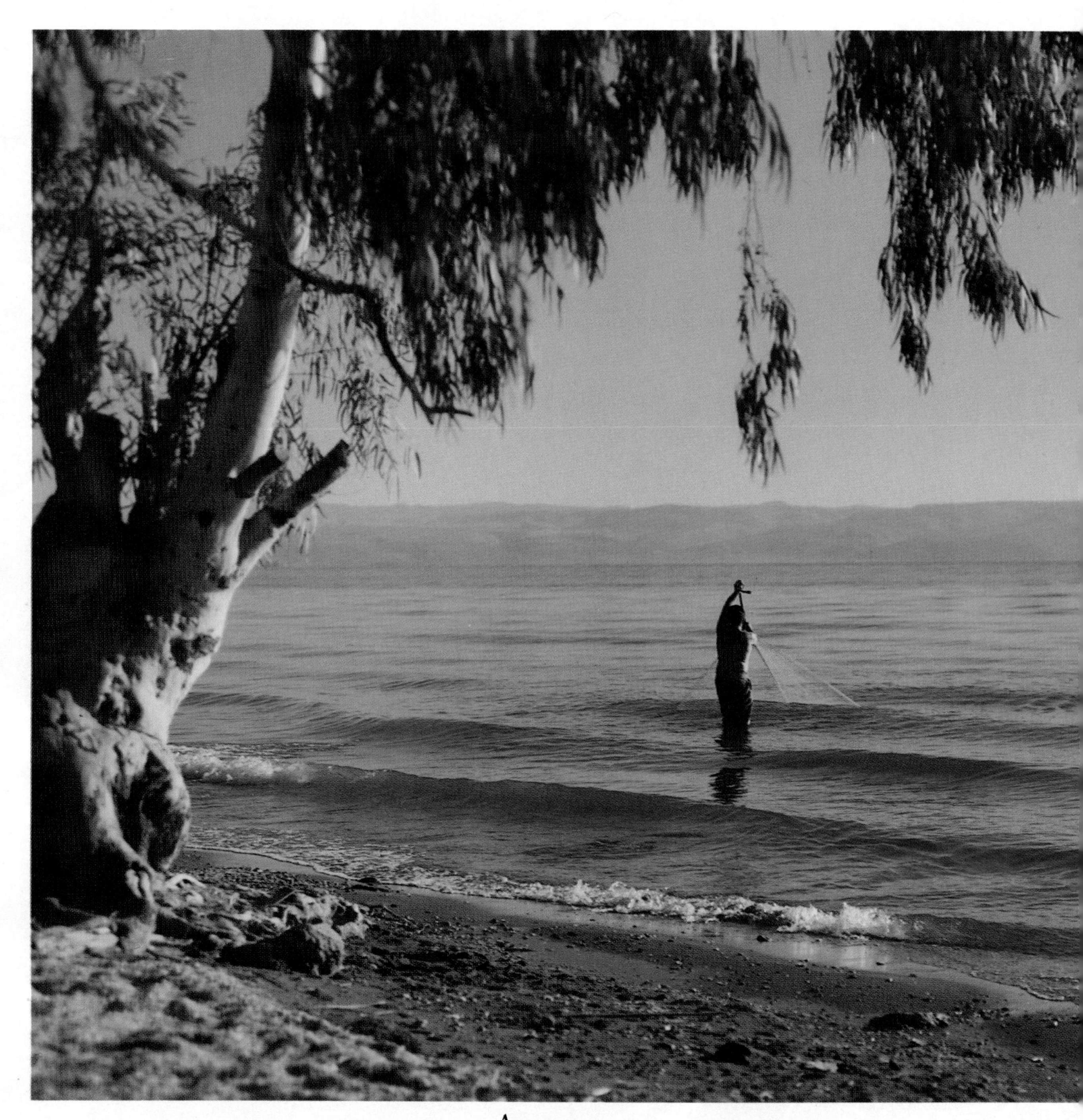

A FISHERMAN using a traditional-style net along the shore of the Sea of Galilee attempts to catch fish as Peter might have done. Fish was a staple food for most of the people in the area and fishing was a thriving industry during Jesus' time. Even today, fishermen use nets like this close to shore where fish gather to feed.

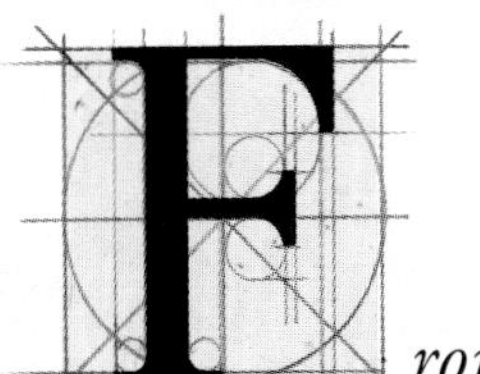

From that time Jesus began to preach, and to say, Repent: for the kingdom of heaven is at hand. And Jesus, walking by the sea of Galilee, saw two brethren, Simon called Peter, and Andrew his brother, casting a net into the sea: for they were fishers. And he saith unto them, Follow me, and I will make you fishers of men. And they straightway left their nets, and followed him.

And going on from thence, he saw other two brethren, James the son of Zebedee, and John his brother, in a ship with Zebedee their father, mending their nets; and he called them. And they immediately left the ship and their father, and followed him.

MATTHEW 4: 17-22

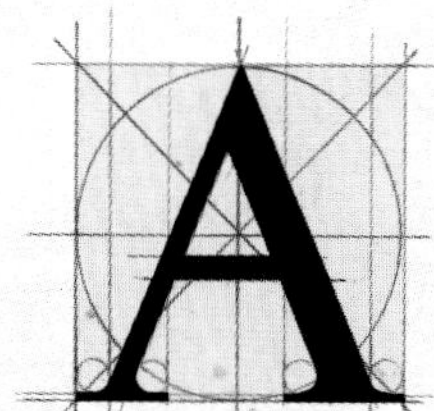

*nd seeing the multitudes, he went up into a mountain . . .
and taught them, saying, Blessed are
the poor in spirit:
for theirs is the kingdom of heaven.
Blessed are they that mourn:
for they shall be comforted.*

*Blessed are the meek:
for they shall inherit the earth.
Blessed are they which do hunger and thirst
after righteousness: for they shall be filled.
Blessed are the merciful:
for they shall obtain mercy.
Blessed are the pure in heart:
for they shall see God.
Blessed are the peacemakers:
for they shall be called the children of God.*

*Blessed are they which are persecuted
for righteousness' sake:
for theirs is the kingdom of heaven.*

MATTHEW 5: 1-10

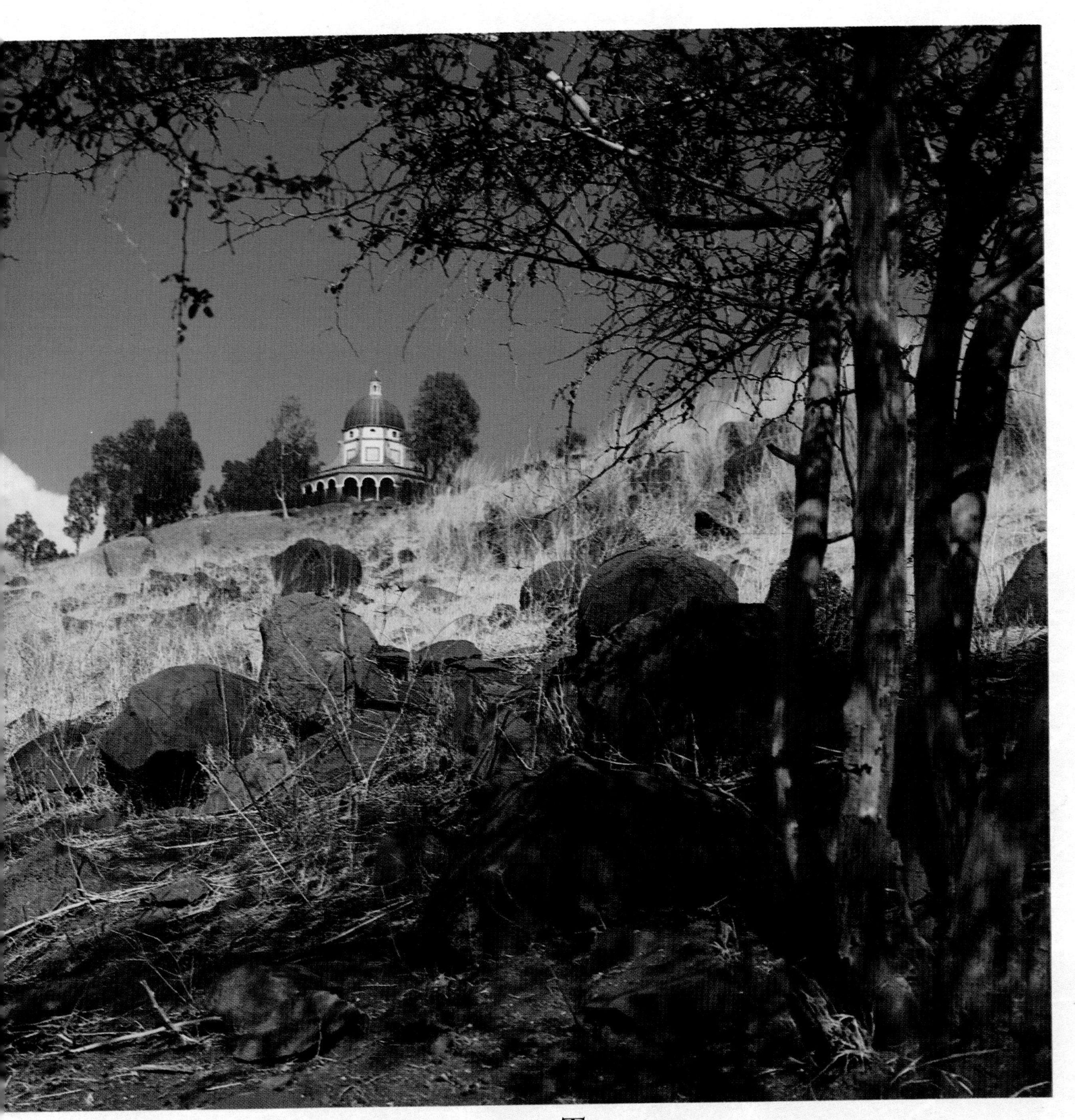

This CHAPEL ON THE MOUNT OF BEATITUDES commemorates Jesus' Sermon on the Mount. The exact site of the sermon is not known, but many scholars believe that it was here, on the northwestern shore of the Sea of Galilee.

Not much remains of this ancient SYNAGOGUE AT CAPERNAUM, built on the site where Jesus frequently preached. Capernaum was located on an important trade route and was a major fishing site on the Sea of Galilee. After Jesus left Nazareth, He made Capernaum the center of much of His ministry.

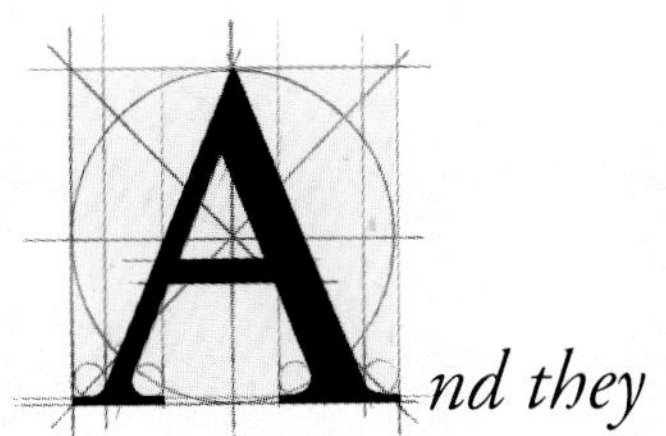

nd they went into Capernaum;
and straightway on the sabbath day
he entered into the synagogue, and taught.
And they were astonished at his doctrine:
for he taught them as one that had authority,
and not as the scribes.

And they were all amazed,
insomuch that they questioned
among themselves, saying,
What thing is this?
what new doctrine is this?
And immediately his fame
spread abroad
throughout all the region
round about Galilee.

MARK 1: 21, 22, 27, 28

When Jesus came
into the coasts of Caesarea Philippi, he
asked his disciples, saying,
Whom do men say that I
the Son of man am? And they said,
Some say that thou art
John the Baptist: some, Elias;
and others, Jeremias,
or one of the prophets.

He saith unto them,
But whom say ye that I am?
And Simon Peter answered
and said,
Thou art the Christ,
the Son of the living God.
And Jesus answered and said unto him,
Blessed art thou, Simon Barjona:
for flesh and blood hath not
revealed it unto thee,
but my Father which is in heaven.

MATTHEW 16: 13-17

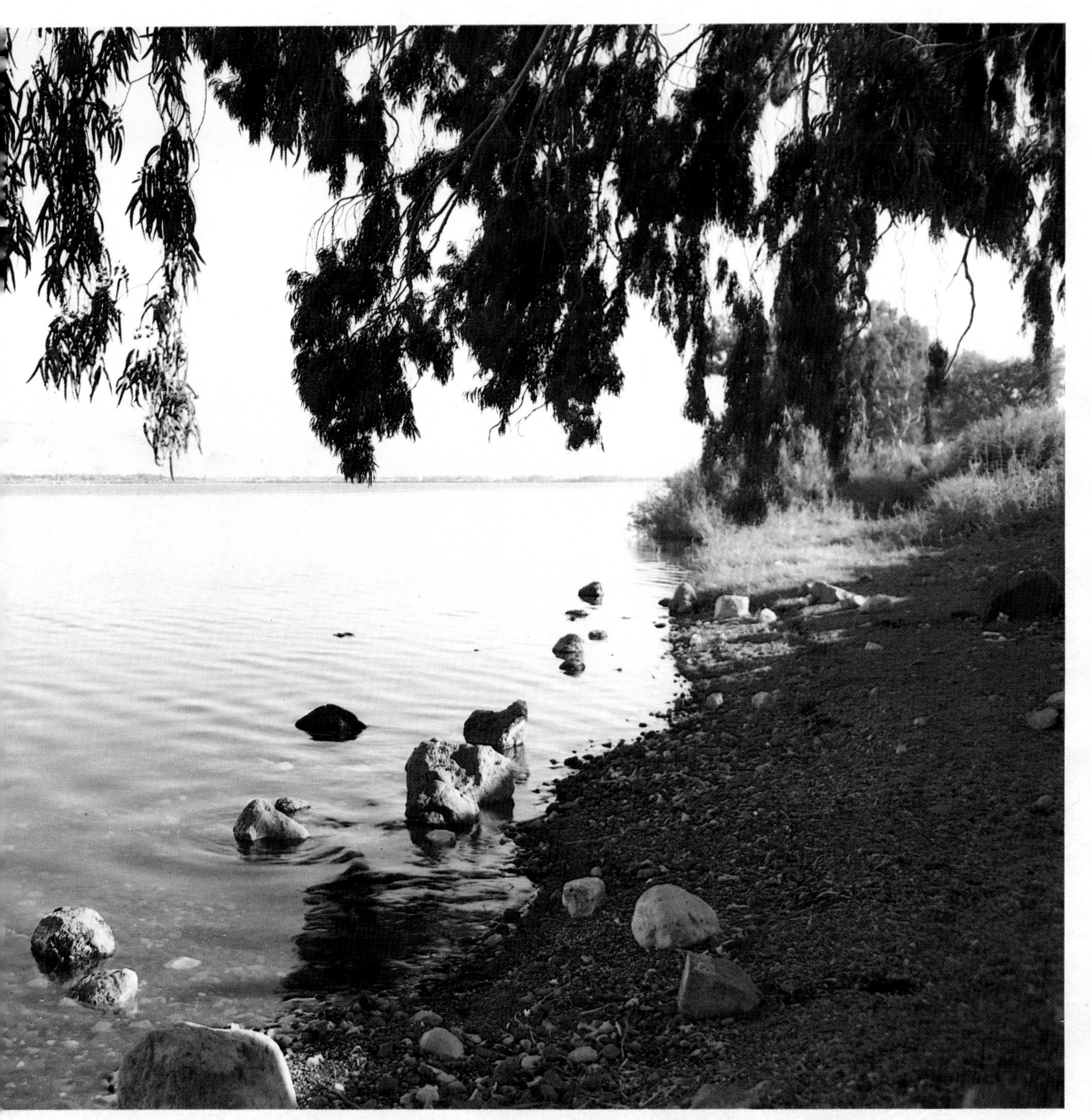

THE SEA OF GALILEE and the area around it were very important in Jesus' ministry. Here He performed eighteen of His thirty-three recorded miracles.

A MOTHER AND HER CHILDREN walk along a road just outside Bethlehem. Even today, the countryside in Israel can be stark and empty.

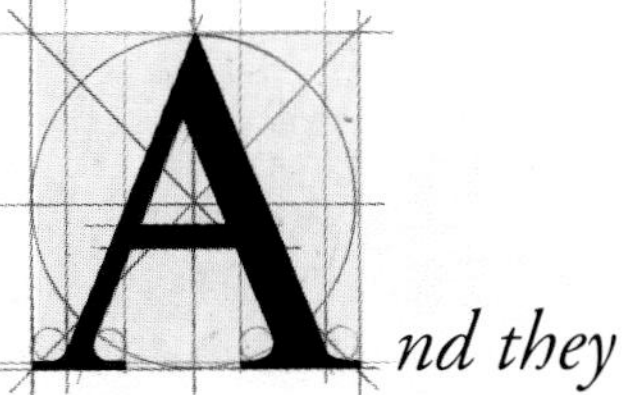

And they brought young children to him,
that he should touch them: and his disciples
rebuked those that brought them.
But when Jesus saw it,
he was much displeased,
and said unto them,
Suffer the little children to come unto me,
and forbid them not:
for of such is the kingdom of God.

Verily I say unto you,
Whosoever shall not receive
the kingdom of God as a little child,
he shall not enter therein.
And he took them up in his arms,
put his hands upon them,
and blessed them.

MARK 10: 13-16

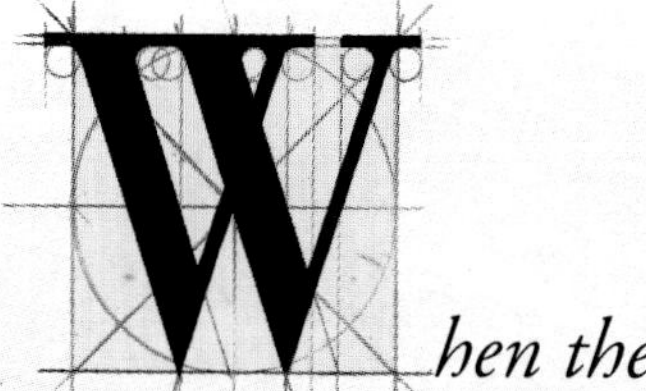hen the
Son of man shall come in his glory. . . . then
shall he sit upon the throne of his glory:
And before him shall be gathered all nations:
and he shall separate them
one from another, as a shepherd divideth
his sheep from the goats. . . .
Then shall the King say unto them . . .
Come, ye blessed of my Father,
inherit the kingdom prepared for you . . .
For I was an hungred, and ye gave me meat:
I was thirsty, and ye gave me drink:
I was a stranger, and ye took me in. . . .
Then shall the righteous answer him,
saying, Lord, when saw we thee an hungred,
and fed thee? or thirsty, and gave thee drink?
And the King shall answer and say unto them,
Verily I say unto you,
Inasmuch as ye have done it
unto one of the least of these my brethren,
ye have done it unto me.

MATTHEW 25: 31, 32, 34-37, 40

Today, as in Biblical times, SHEEP AND GOATS graze on Israeli hillsides. Most Biblical scholars believe this hill, northwest of the Sea of Galilee and just south of Capernaum, is the site of the Sermon on the Mount.

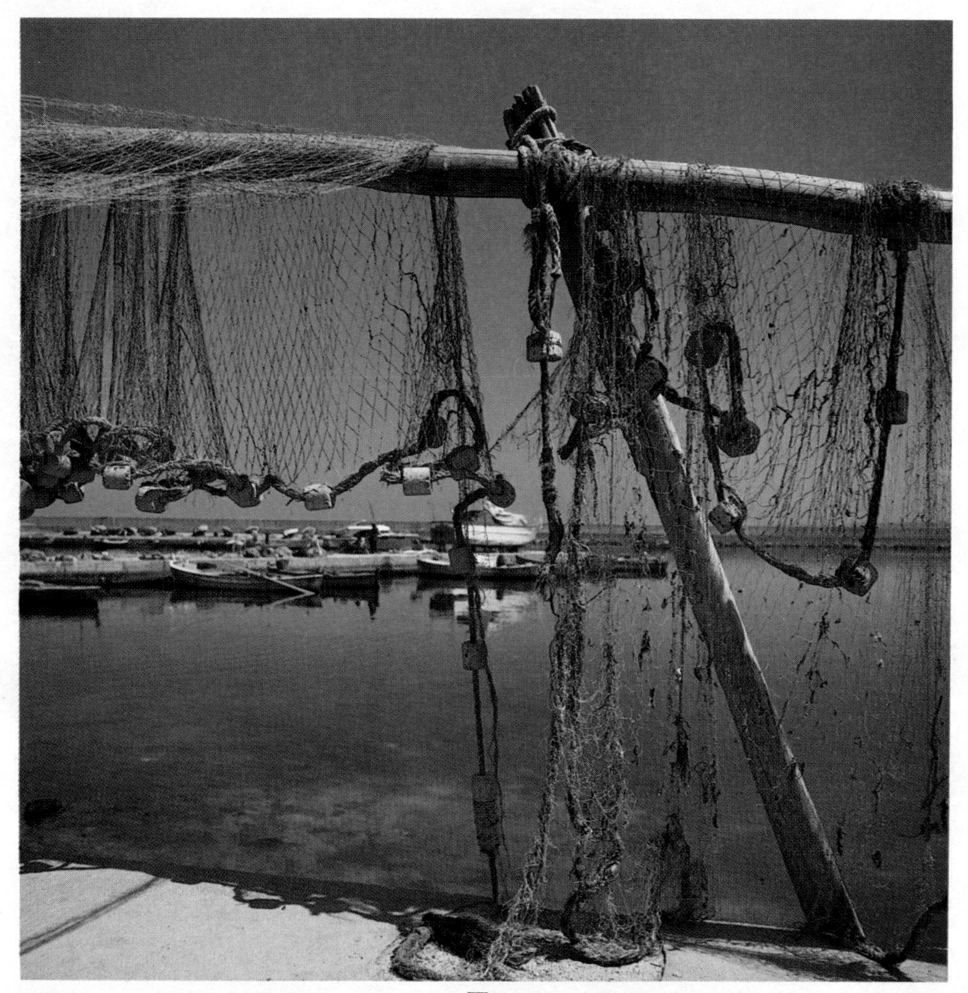

FISHING BOATS line up at the dock at the ancient city of Tyre on the Mediterranean Sea. Although Peter lived and worked on the Sea of Galilee, he may have used nets and boats similar to some of those pictured here.

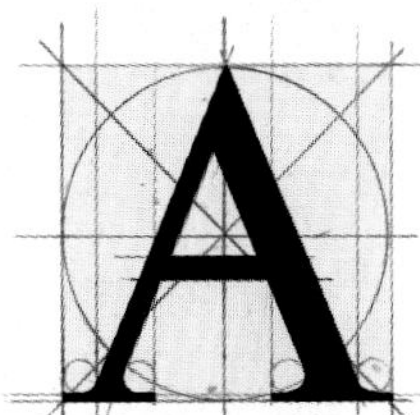

*nd I say also
unto thee, that thou art Peter, and upon this
rock I will build my church;
and the gates of hell shall not prevail against it.
And I will give unto thee
the keys of the kingdom of heaven:
and whatsoever thou shalt bind on earth
shall be bound in heaven:
and whatsoever thou shalt loose on earth
shall be loosed in heaven.
If any man will come after me,
let him deny himself, and take up his cross,
and follow me. For whosoever will save his
life shall lose it: and whosoever will lose
his life for my sake shall find it.
For what is a man profited,
if he shall gain the whole world,
and lose his own soul?
For the Son of man shall come in the glory
of his Father with his angels;
and then he shall reward every man
according to his works.*

MATTHEW 16: 18, 19, 24-27

nd it came to pass, when Jesus had made an end of commanding his twelve disciples, he departed thence to teach and to preach in their cities.

Then began he to upbraid the cities wherein most of his mighty works were done, because they repented not:

Woe unto thee, Chorazin! Woe unto thee, Bethsaida! for if the mighty works, which were done in you, had been done in Tyre and Sidon, they would have repented long ago in sackcloth and ashes. But I say unto you, It shall be more tolerable for Tyre and Sidon at the day of judgement, than for you.

MATTHEW 11: 1, 20-22

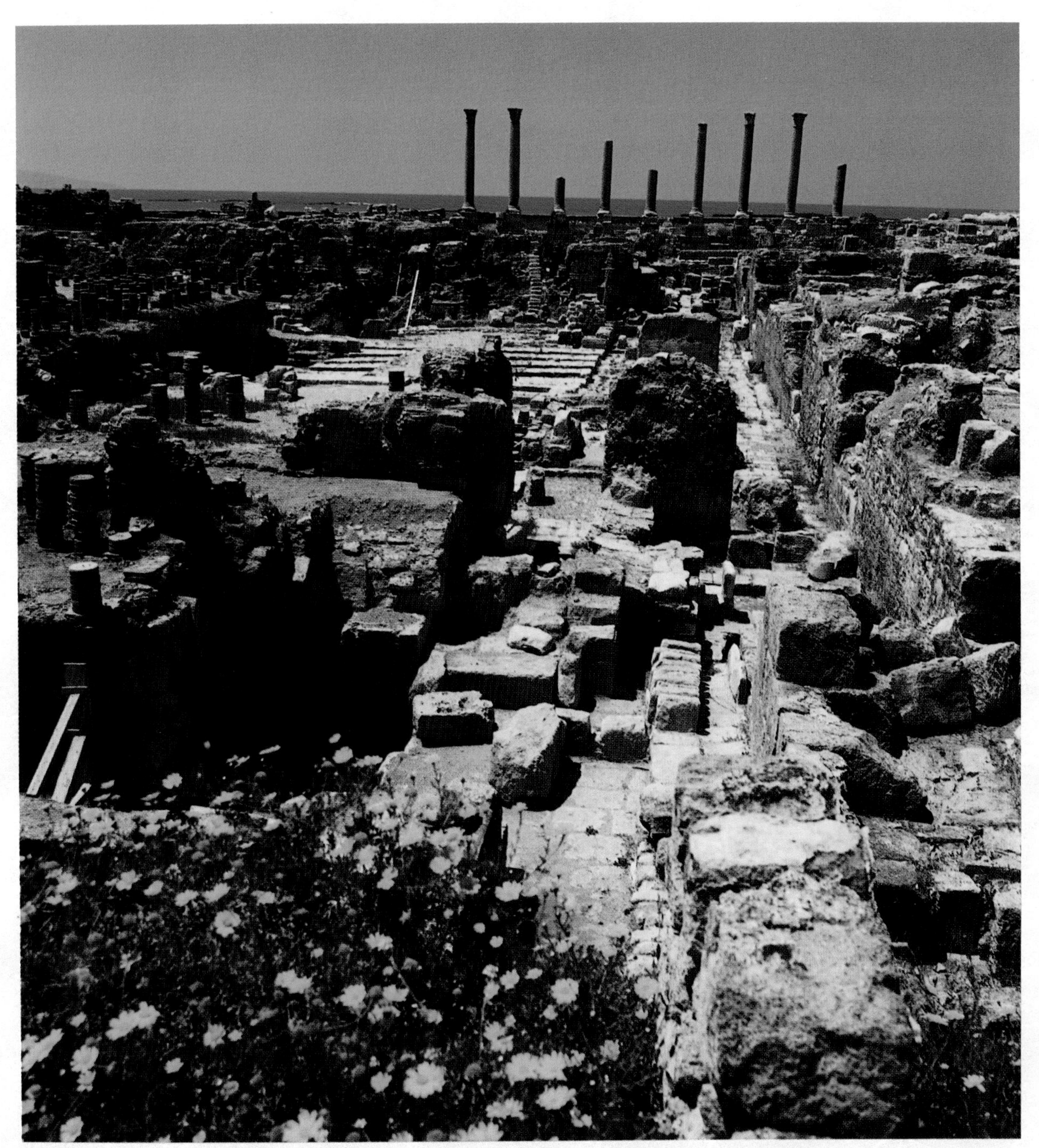

The ancient Phoenicians founded TYRE as a principle seaport, possibly as early as 2750 B.C. When Jesus traveled through this region, the city was experiencing a renewed period of prosperity. Later, Paul often visited a flourishing Christian community at Tyre.

Some Biblical scholars believe the word "lily" is a generic term for flowers in general. These LILIES, with rosy, pink blossoms, grow abundantly in the fields throughout Israel and Jordan.

*Consider the
lilies of the field, how they grow;
they toil not, neither do they spin:
And yet I say unto you,
That even Solomon in all his glory
was not arrayed like one of these.
Wherefore, if God so clothe
the grass of the field,
which today is, and tomorrow
is cast into the oven,
shall he not much more clothe you,
O ye of little faith?*

*Therefore take no thought, saying,
What shall we eat? or, What shall we drink?
or, Wherewithal shall we be clothed?
But seek ye first the kingdom of God,
and his righteousness;
and all these things
shall be added unto you.*

MATTHEW 6: 28-31, 33

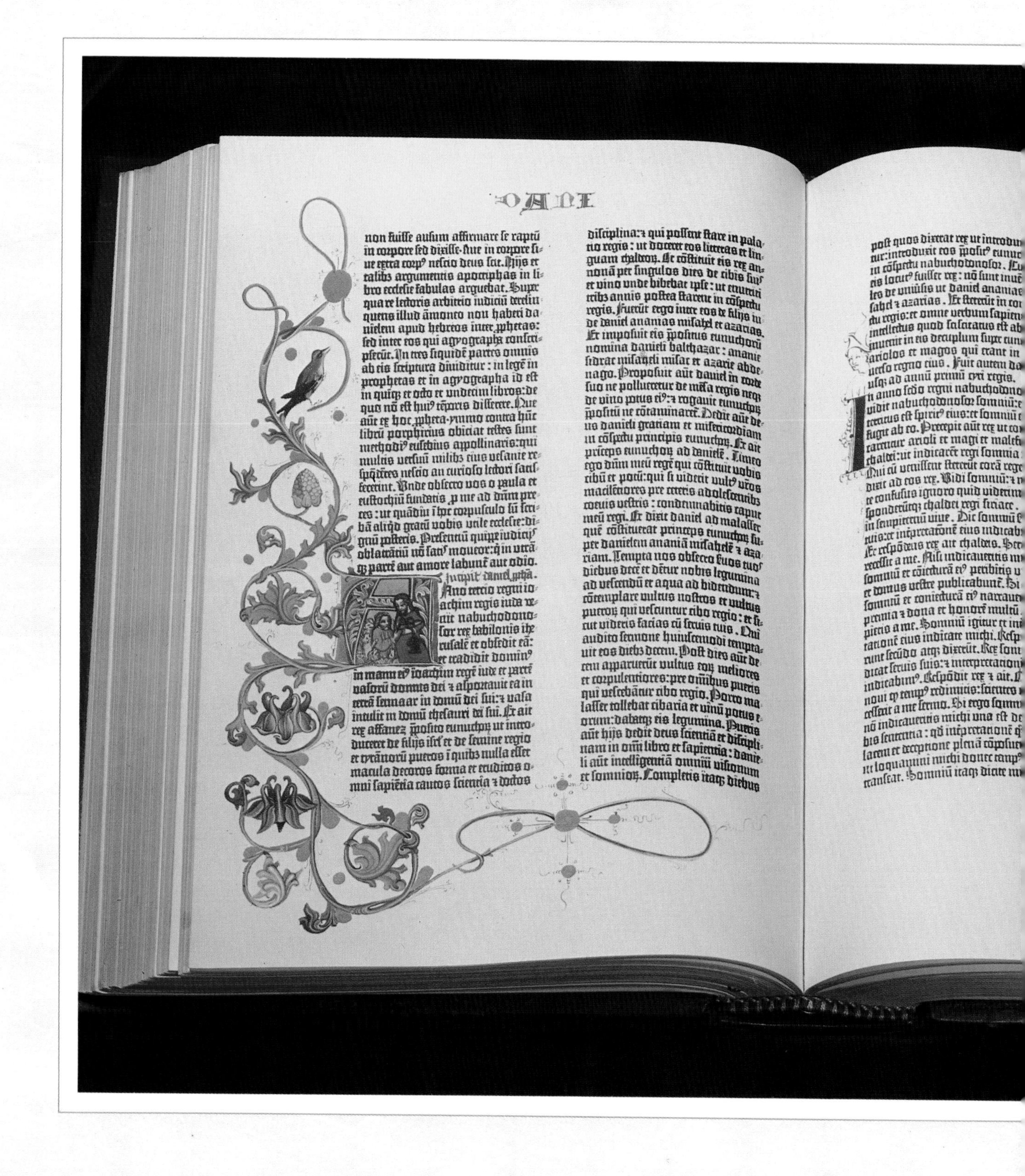

THE PARABLES

*urely he*

hath borne our griefs,

and carried our sorrows:

yet we did esteem him stricken,

smitten of God, and afflicted.

ISAIAH 53: 4

Prior to the invention of movable type, hand-copied books and Bibles were available only to a select few. The publication of the GUTENBERG BIBLE in 1456 by German printer Johann Gutenberg led to the future of mass publication, making books and Bibles more accessible to the common person. A facsimile of a Gutenberg Bible is pictured.

Primitive farming methods are still in use today in much of the Middle East. Here, a JORDANIAN FARMER plows his field in the ancient manner with the aid of a team of oxen.

Behold, a sower went forth to sow. . . . some seeds fell by the way side, and the fowls . . . devoured them up. . . . And some fell among thorns; and the thorns . . . choked them: But other fell into good ground, and brought forth fruit. . . .
And the disciples came, and said unto him, Why speakest thou unto them in parables?
He answered and said unto them, Because it is given unto you to know the mysteries of the kingdom of heaven, but to them it is not given.
For whosoever hath, to him shall be given, and he shall have more abundance: but whosoever hath not, from him shall be taken away even that he hath. For verily I say unto you, That many prophets and righteous men have desired to see those things which ye see, and have not seen them; and to hear those things which ye hear, and have not heard them.

MATTHEW 13: 3, 4, 7, 8, 10-12, 17

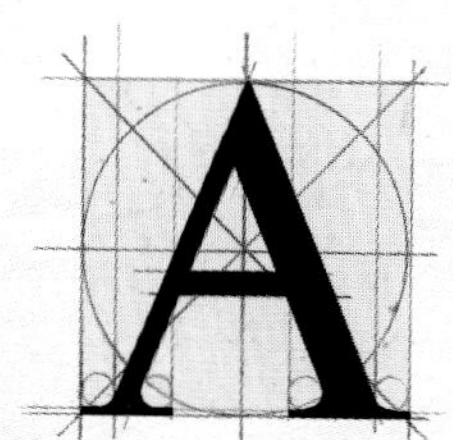

A certain man went down from Jerusalem to Jericho, and fell among thieves, which stripped him of his raiment, and wounded him, and departed, leaving him half dead. And by chance there came down a certain priest that way. . . . And likewise a Levite . . . and looked on him, and passed by. . . .

But a certain Samaritan, as he journeyed, came where he was: and when he saw him, he had compassion on him, And went to him, and bound up his wounds, pouring in oil and wine, and set him on his own beast, and brought him to an inn, and took care of him.

Which now of these three, thinkest thou, was neighbour unto him that fell among the thieves? Then said Jesus . . . Go, and do thou likewise.

LUKE 10: 30-34, 36, 37

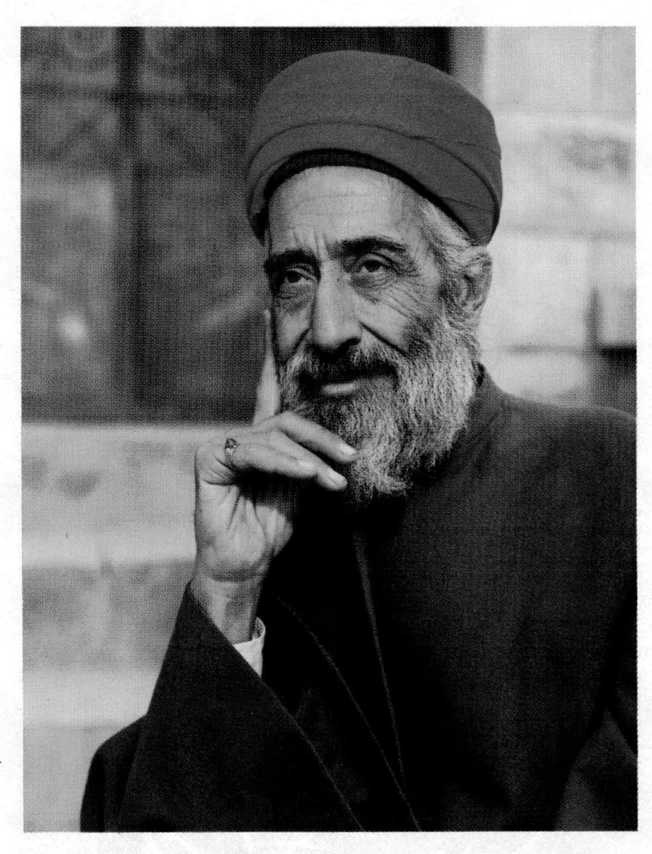

The SAMARITANS were once a proud and prolific people. Today they number fewer than one hundred and fifty.

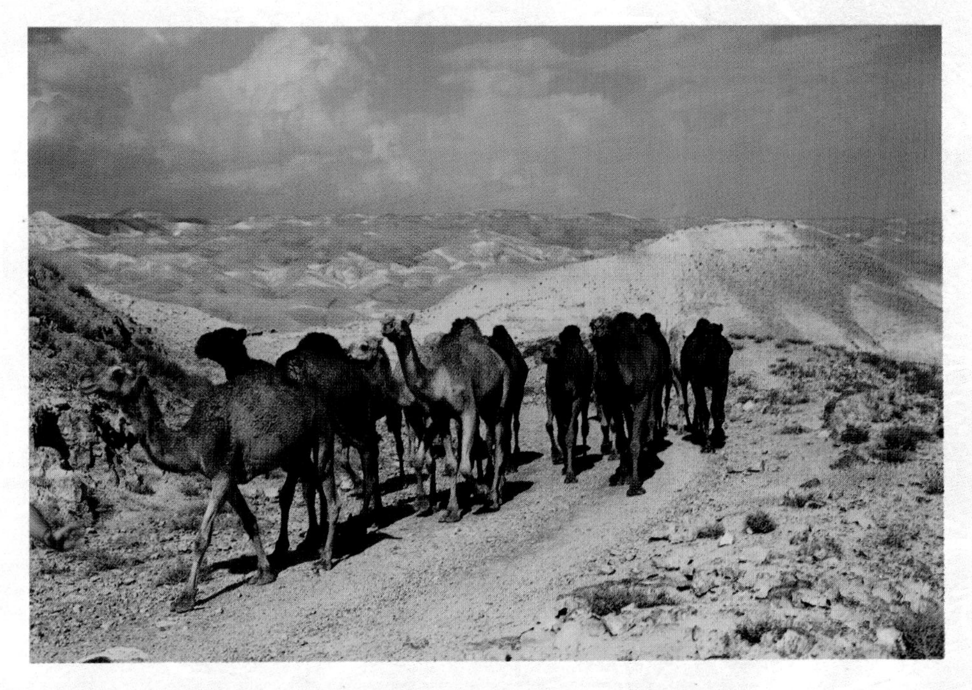

A CAMEL CARAVAN travels along an old Roman road between Jericho and Jerusalem. It is along such a road that the "Good Samaritan" found and cared for his injured fellowman.

Living a life that has changed little over the centuries, a SHEPHERD keeps watch over his sheep on a rocky hillside near the ruins of the ancient city of Ephesus in modern-day Turkey.

What man
of you, having an hundred sheep,
if he lose one of them,
doth not leave the ninety and nine
in the wilderness,
and go after that which is lost,
until he find it?

And when he hath found it,
he layeth it on his shoulders, rejoicing.
And when he cometh home,
he calleth together his friends
and neighbours, saying unto them,
Rejoice with me;
for I have found my sheep which was lost.

I say unto you, that likewise
joy shall be in heaven over one sinner
that repenteth, more than over ninety
and nine just persons,
which need no repentance.

LUKE 15: 4-7

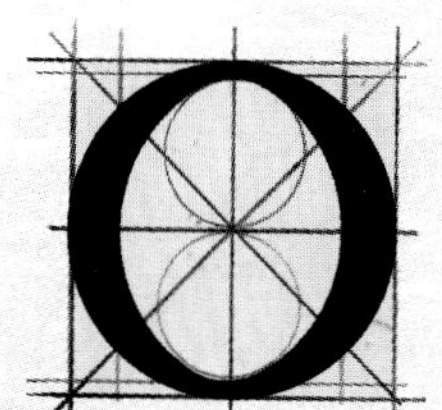

ne came and said unto him, Good Master, what good things shall I do, that I may have eternal life? And he said unto him . . . if thou wilt enter into life, keep the commandments.
The young man saith unto him, All these things have I kept from my youth up: what lack I yet?

Jesus said unto him, If thou wilt be perfect, go and sell that thou hast, and give to the poor, and thou shalt have treasure in heaven: and come and follow me.

Then said Jesus unto his disciples, Verily I say unto you, that a rich man shall hardly enter into the kingdom of heaven. And again I say unto you, It is easier for a camel to go through the eye of a needle, than for a rich man to enter into the kingdom of God.

MATTHEW 19: 16, 17, 20, 21, 23, 24

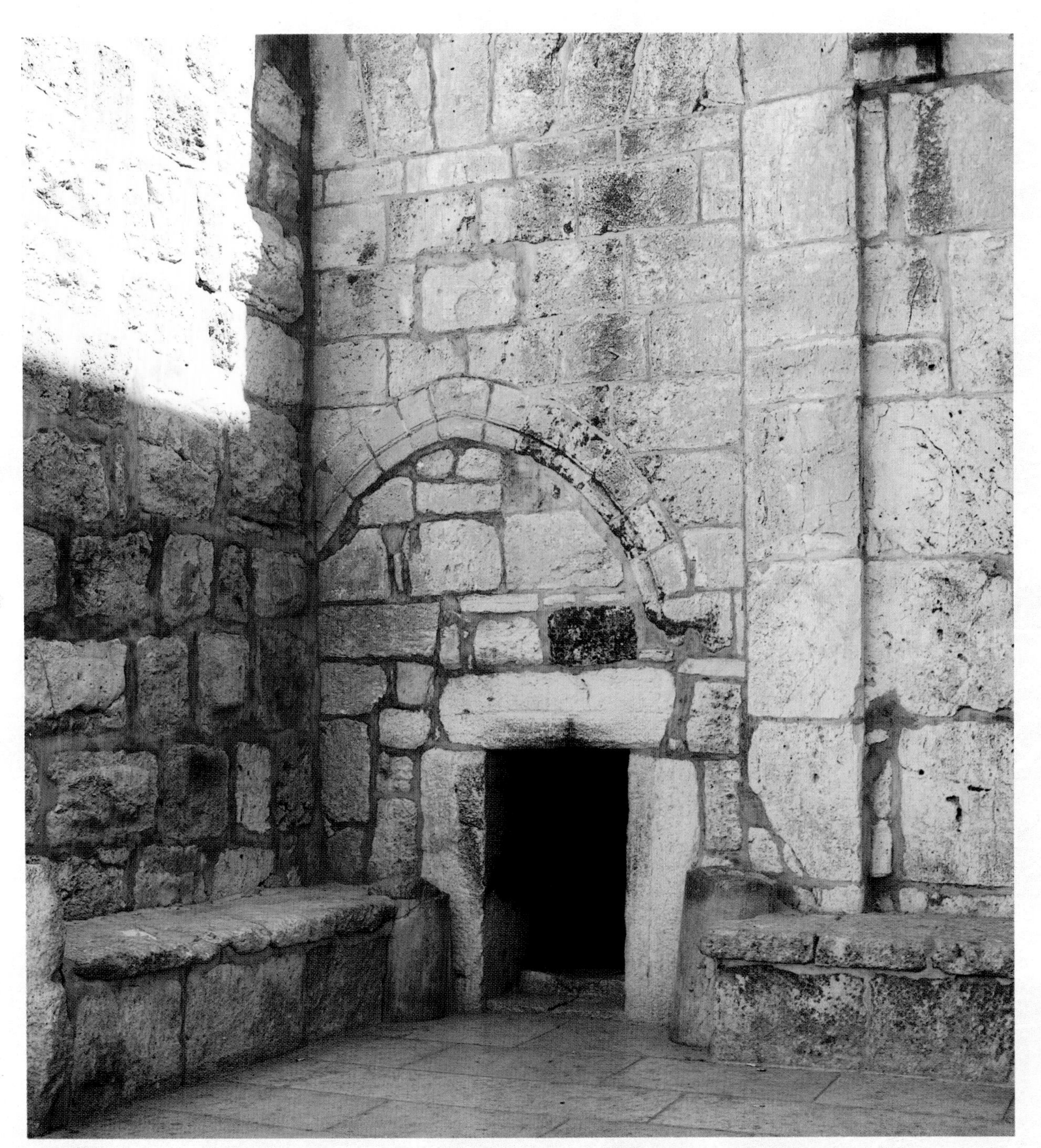

THE EYE OF THE NEEDLE GATE into The Church of the Nativity in Bethlehem is cited by some scholars as Jesus' reference in the parable. A fully loaded camel could only pass through this narrow gate with great difficulty and only after all of its load was removed.

Large, luscious CLUSTERS OF GRAPES are common in Israel, where the soil and climate are well-suited to vineyards. Grapes were cultivated in the area long before the Israelites occupied the land, and are mentioned frequently in the Old and New Testaments.

*I am the true
vine, and my Father is the husbandman.
Every branch in me that beareth not fruit
he taketh away: and every branch
that beareth fruit, he purgeth it,
that it may bring forth more fruit.
Now ye are clean through the
word which I have spoken unto you.
I am the vine, ye are the branches:
He that abideth in me, and I in him,
the same bringeth forth much fruit:
for without me ye can do nothing.
If ye abide in me, and my words
abide in you, ye shall ask what
ye will, and it shall be done unto you.
Herein is my Father glorified,
that ye bear much fruit; so shall ye be my
disciples. As the Father hath loved me,
so have I loved you:
continue ye in my love.*

JOHN 15: 1-3, 5-9

He that entereth not by the door into the sheepfold, but climbeth up some other way, the same is a thief and a robber. But he that entereth in by the door is the shepherd of the sheep. To him the porter openeth. . . . And when he putteth forth his own sheep, he goeth before them, and the sheep follow him. . . . I am the good shepherd: the good shepherd giveth his life for the sheep. As the Father knoweth me, even so know I the Father: and I lay down my life for the sheep. And other sheep I have, which are not of this fold: them also I must bring, and they shall hear my voice; and there shall be one fold, and one shepherd. Therefore doth my Father love me, because I lay down my life, that I might take it again. I have power to lay it down, and I have power to take it again. This commandment have I received of my Father.

JOHN 10: 1-4, 11, 15-18

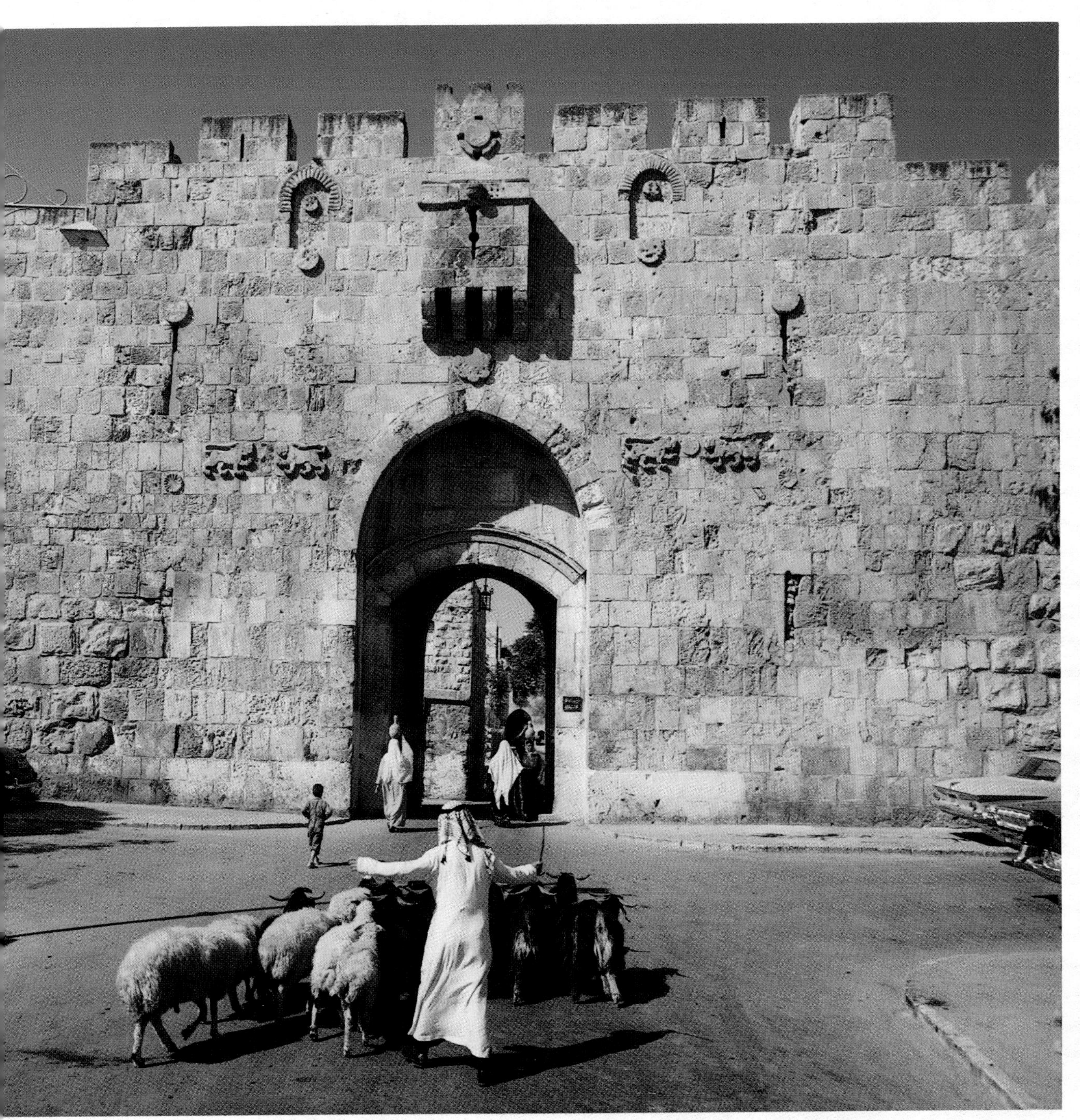

Traffic still flows through ST. STEPHEN'S GATE into the walled city of Jerusalem. Stephen, one of the first seven leaders of the early church, was stoned to death after he reported a vision of God with Jesus on His right hand. Saul, later to be called Paul, watched over the cloaks of those who threw the stones. Stephen's martyrdom led to the persecution of the disciples, forcing them to flee Jerusalem into other areas.

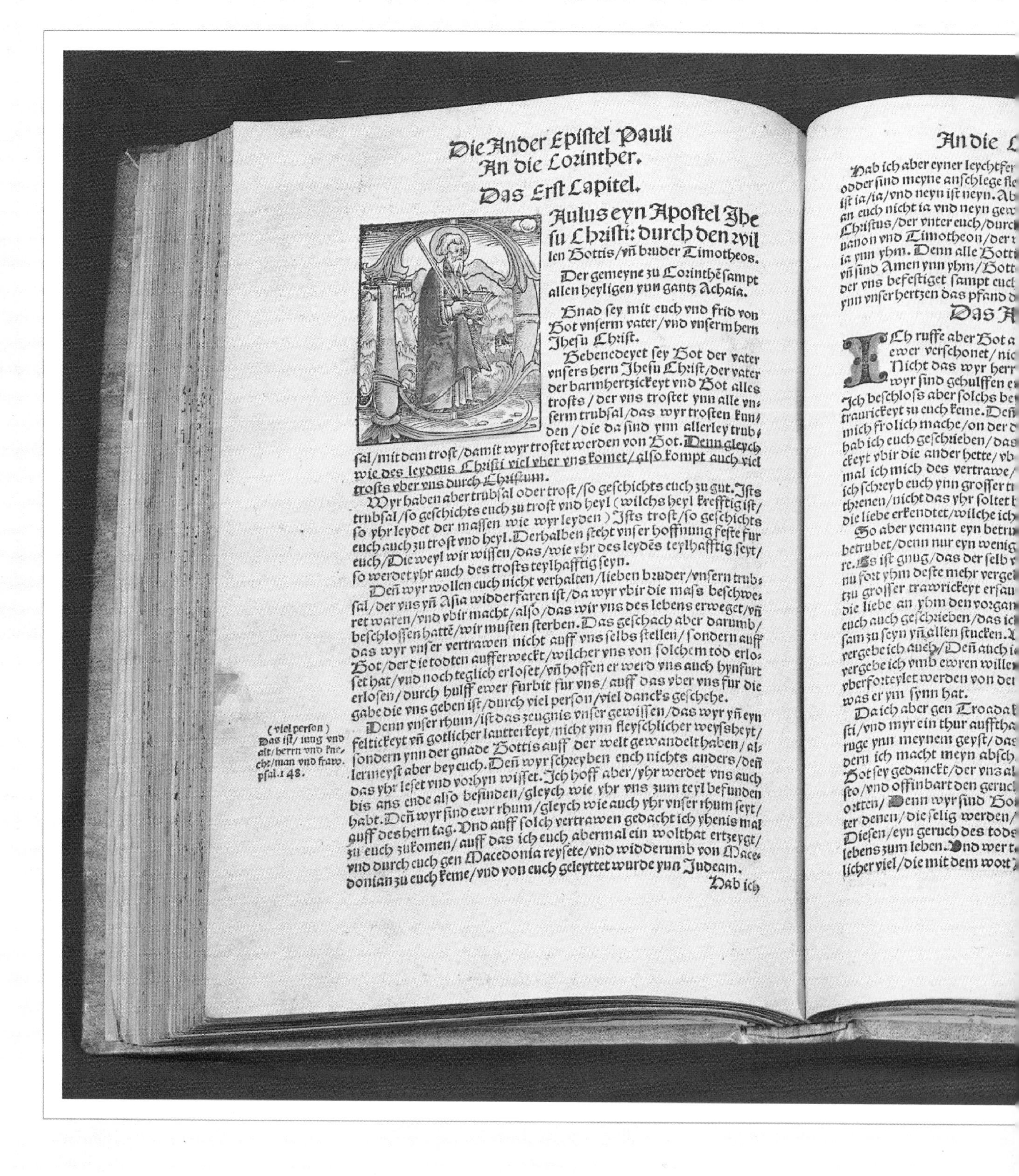

Die Ander Epistel Pauli
An die Corinther.
Das Erst Capitel.

Aulus eyn Apostel Jhe
su Christi: durch den wil
len Gottis/vñ bruder Timotheos.

Der gemeyne zu Corinthē sampt
allen heyligen ynn gantz Achaia.

Gnad sey mit euch vnd frid von
Got vnserm vater/vnd vnserm hern
Jhesu Christ.

Gebenedeyet sey Got der vater
vnsers hern Jhesu Christ/der vater
der barmhertzickeyt vnd Got alles
trosts / der vns trostet ynn alle vnserm trubsal/das wyr trosten kun-
den / die da sind ynn allerley trub-
sal/mit dem trost/damit wyr trostet werden von Got. Denn gleych
wie des leydens Christi viel vber vns komet/also kompt auch viel
trosts vber vns durch Christum.

Wyr haben aber trubsal oder trost/so geschichts euch zu gut. Ists
trubsal/so geschichts euch zu trost vnd heyl (wilchs heyl krefftig ist/
so yhr leydet der massen wie wyr leyden) Ists trost/so geschichts
euch auch zu trost vnd heyl. Derhalben steht vnser hoffnung feste fur
euch/Die weyl wir wissen/das/wie yhr des leydēs teylhafftig seyt/
so werdet yhr auch des trosts teylhafftig seyn.

Deñ wyr wollen euch nicht verhalten/lieben bruder/vnsern trub-
sal/der vns yñ Asia widderfaren ist/da wyr vbir die mass beschwe-
ret waren/vnd vbir macht/also/das wir vns des lebens erweget/vñ
beschlossen hattē/wir musten sterben. Das geschach aber darumb/
das wyr vnser vertrawen nicht auff vns selbs stellen/sondern auff
Got/der die todten aufferweckt/wilcher vns von solchem tod erlo-
set hat/vnd noch teglich erloset/vñ hoffen er werd vns auch hynfurt
erlosen/durch hulff ewer furbit fur vns/auff das vber vns fur die
gabe die vns geben ist/durch viel person/viel dancks geschehe.

Denn vnser rhum/ist das zeugnis vnser gewissen/das wyr yñ eyn
feltickeyt vñ gotlicher lautterkeyt/nicht ynn fleyschlicher weysheyt/
sondern ynn der gnade Gottis auff der welt gewandelt haben/al-
lermeyst aber bey euch. Deñ wyr schreyben euch nichts anders/deñ
das yhr leset vnd vorhyn wisset. Ich hoff aber/yhr werdet vns auch
bis ans ende also befinden/gleych wie yhr vns zum teyl befunden
habt. Deñ wyr sind ewr rhum/gleych wie auch yhr vnser rhum seyt/
auff des hern tag. Vnd auff solch vertrawen gedacht ich yhenis mal
zu euch zukomen/auff das ich euch abermal ein wolthat ertzeygt/
vnd durch euch gen Macedonia reysete/vnd widderumb von Mace-
donian zu euch keme/vnd von euch geleyttet wurde ynn Judeam.

(viel person) Das ist/iung vnd alt/herrn vnd knecht/man vnd fraw. psal. 148.

Hab ich

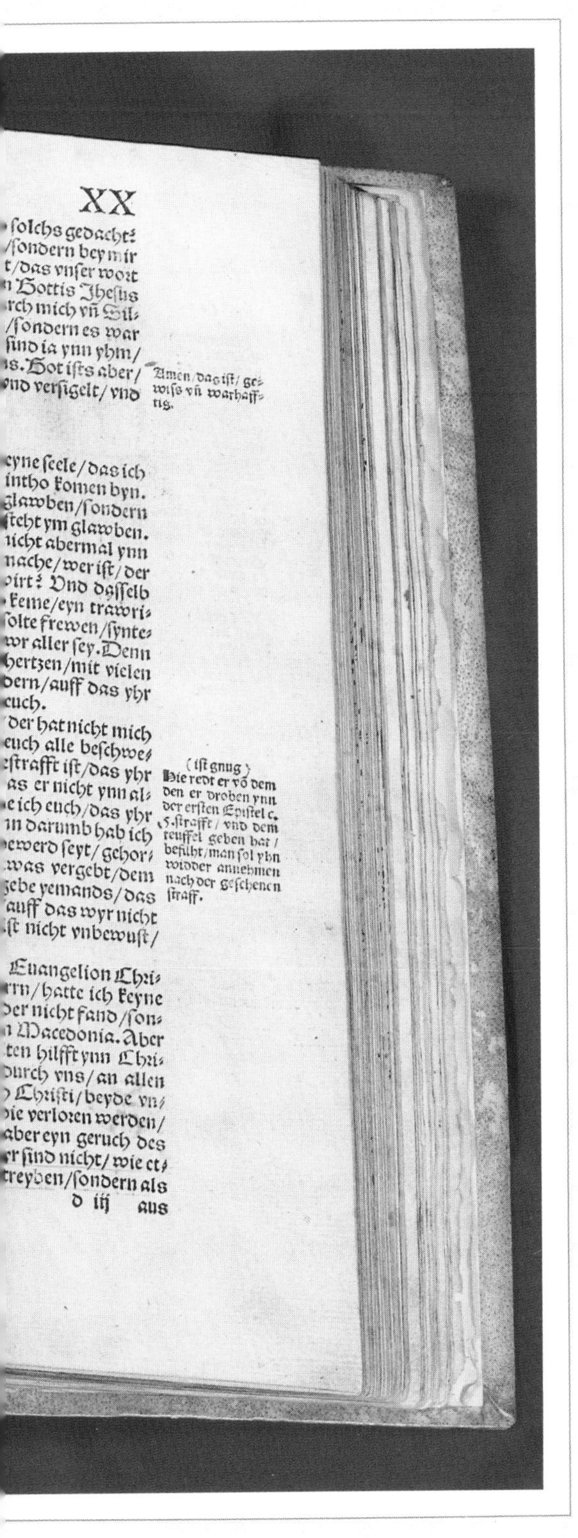

XX
folchs gedacht?
/sondern bey mir
t/das vnser wort
n Gottis Jhesus
rch mich vñ Sil-
/sondern es war
sind ia ynn yhm/
ıs. Got ists aber/
vnd versigelt/ vnd

Amen/das ist/ gewiss vñ warhafftig.

eyne seele/das ich
intho komen byn.
glawben/sondern
steht ym glawben.
nicht abermal ynn
nache/wer ist/der
virt? Vnd dasselb
keme/eyn trawri-
solte frewen/synte-
wr aller sey. Denn
hertzen/mit vielen
dern/auff das yhr
euch.
der hat nicht mich
euch alle beschwe-
estrafft ist/das yhr
as er nicht ynn al-
e ich euch/das yhr
in darumb hab ich
ewerd seyt/gehor-
was vergebt/dem
gebe yemands/das
auff das wyr nicht
st nicht vnbewust/

(ist gnug) Hie redt er vō dem den er droben ynn der ersten Epistel c. 5. strafft/ vnd dem teuffel geben hat/ befilht/man sol yhn widder annehmen nach der geschenen straff.

Euangelion Chri-
rrn/hatte ich keyne
der nicht fand/son-
n Macedonia. Aber
ten hilfft ynn Chri-
durch vns/an allen
Christi/beyde vn-
die verloren werden/
aber eyn geruch des
er sind nicht/wie et-
treyben/sondern als
d iij aus

THE MIRACLES

*ing,*

O heavens; and be joyful, O earth;

and break forth into singing,

O mountains:

for the LORD hath comforted

his people, and will have mercy

upon his afflicted.

ISAIAH 49: 13

In 1517, German reformer Martin Luther tacked his ninety-five theses on the cathedral door in Wittenburg, denying final papal authority in Bible interpretation, declaring the "priesthood of all believers," and denying transubstantiation in favor of consubstantiation. Protected by Frederick III of Saxony, Luther translated the New Testament into German, completing this awesome task in only six months. The MARTIN LUTHER NEW TESTAMENT pictured dates from 1525.

The village of CANA, the site of Jesus' first miracle, is situated a few miles north of Nazareth. In excavated homes in Cana, archaeologists have found remains of stone jars similar to those mentioned in the Book of John.

And the third day there was a marriage in Cana of Galilee; and the mother of Jesus was there: And both Jesus was called, and his disciples, to the marriage. And when they wanted wine, the mother of Jesus saith unto him, They have no wine. Jesus saith unto her, Woman, what have I to do with thee? mine hour is not yet come. His mother saith unto the servants, Whatsoever he saith unto you, do it. Jesus saith unto them, Fill the waterpots with water. And they filled them up to the brim. And he saith unto them, Draw out now, and bear unto the governor of the feast. And they bare it. When the ruler of the feast had tasted the water that was made wine. . . . the governor of the feast called the bridegroom, And saith unto him, Every man at the beginning doth set forth good wine . . . but thou hast kept the good wine until now. This beginning of miracles did Jesus in Cana of Galilee, and manifested forth his glory; and his disciples believed on him.

JOHN 2: 1-5, 7-11

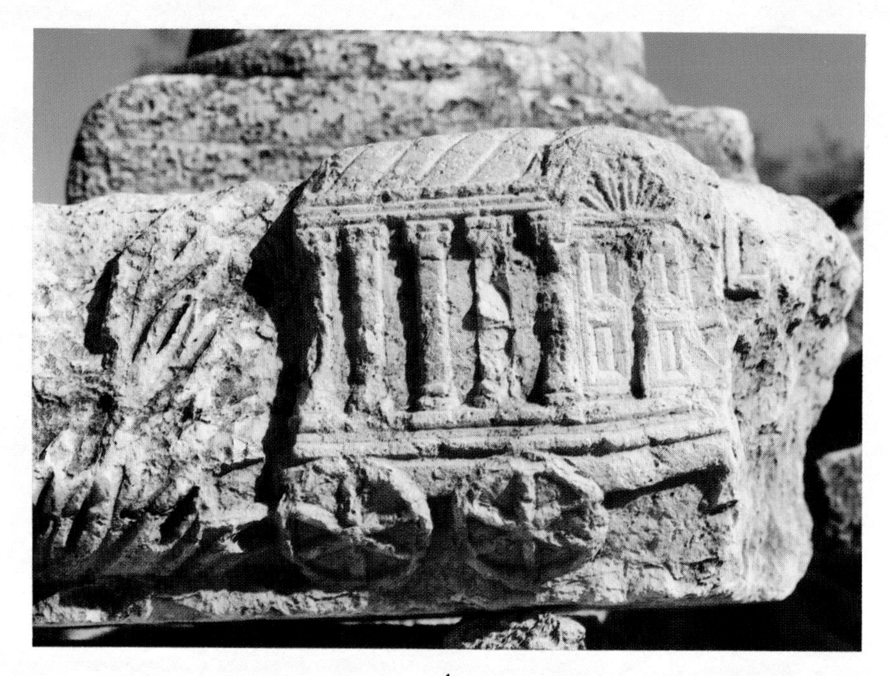

At these ruins of a SYNAGOGUE IN CAPERNAUM, intricate stone work combines Roman architectural styles with a representation of the Jewish Ark of the Covenant. This synagogue was most likely built by Roman soldiers in the third century; however, Christ is thought to have preached frequently at an earlier synagogue on this site.

And, behold,
they brought to him a man sick of
the palsy, lying on a bed:
and Jesus seeing their faith said . . .
Son, be of good cheer;
thy sins be forgiven thee.
And, behold, certain of the scribes
said within themselves, This man
blasphemeth. And Jesus
knowing their thoughts said,
Wherefore think ye evil in your hearts?
For whether is easier, to say,
Thy sins be forgiven thee;
or to say, Arise, and walk?
But that ye may know that the Son of man
hath power on earth to forgive sins,
(then saith he to the sick of the palsy,)
Arise, take up thy bed. . . .
And he arose, and departed to his house.
But when the multitudes saw it,
they marvelled, and glorified God,
which had given such power unto men.

MATTHEW 9: 2-8

Jesus spent a few days in the small village of SYCHAR in Samaria during his ministry. Located here is Jacob's Well, where Jesus spoke with the Samarian woman.

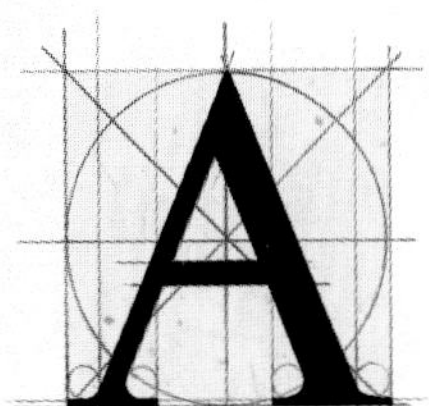

And as he entered into a certain village, there met him ten men that were lepers, which stood afar off: And they lifted up their voices, and said, Jesus, Master, have mercy on us. And when he saw them, he said unto them, Go shew yourselves unto the priests. And it came to pass, that, as they went, they were cleansed. And one of them, when he saw that he was healed, turned back, and with a loud voice glorified God, And fell down on his face at his feet, giving him thanks. . . .

And Jesus answering said, were there not ten cleansed? but where are the nine? There are not found that returned to give glory to God, save this stranger. And he said unto him, Arise, go thy way: thy faith hath made thee whole.

LUKE 17: 12-19

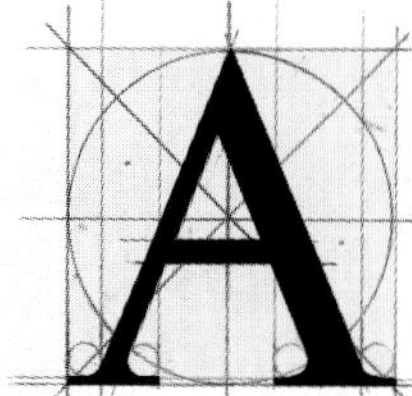

nd as Jesus
passed by, he saw a man which was
blind from his birth. And his disciples asked
him, saying, Master, who did sin, this man,
or his parents, that he was born blind?
Jesus answered, Neither hath this man sinned,
nor his parents: but that the works
of God should be made manifest
in him. I must work the works
of him that sent me, while it is day:
the night cometh, when no man can work.
As long as I am in the world,
I am the light of the world.

When he had thus spoken, he spat on the
ground . . . and he anointed the eyes of the
blind man . . . And said unto him,
Go, wash in the pool of Siloam. . . .
He went his way therefore, and washed,
and came seeing.

JOHN 9: 1-7

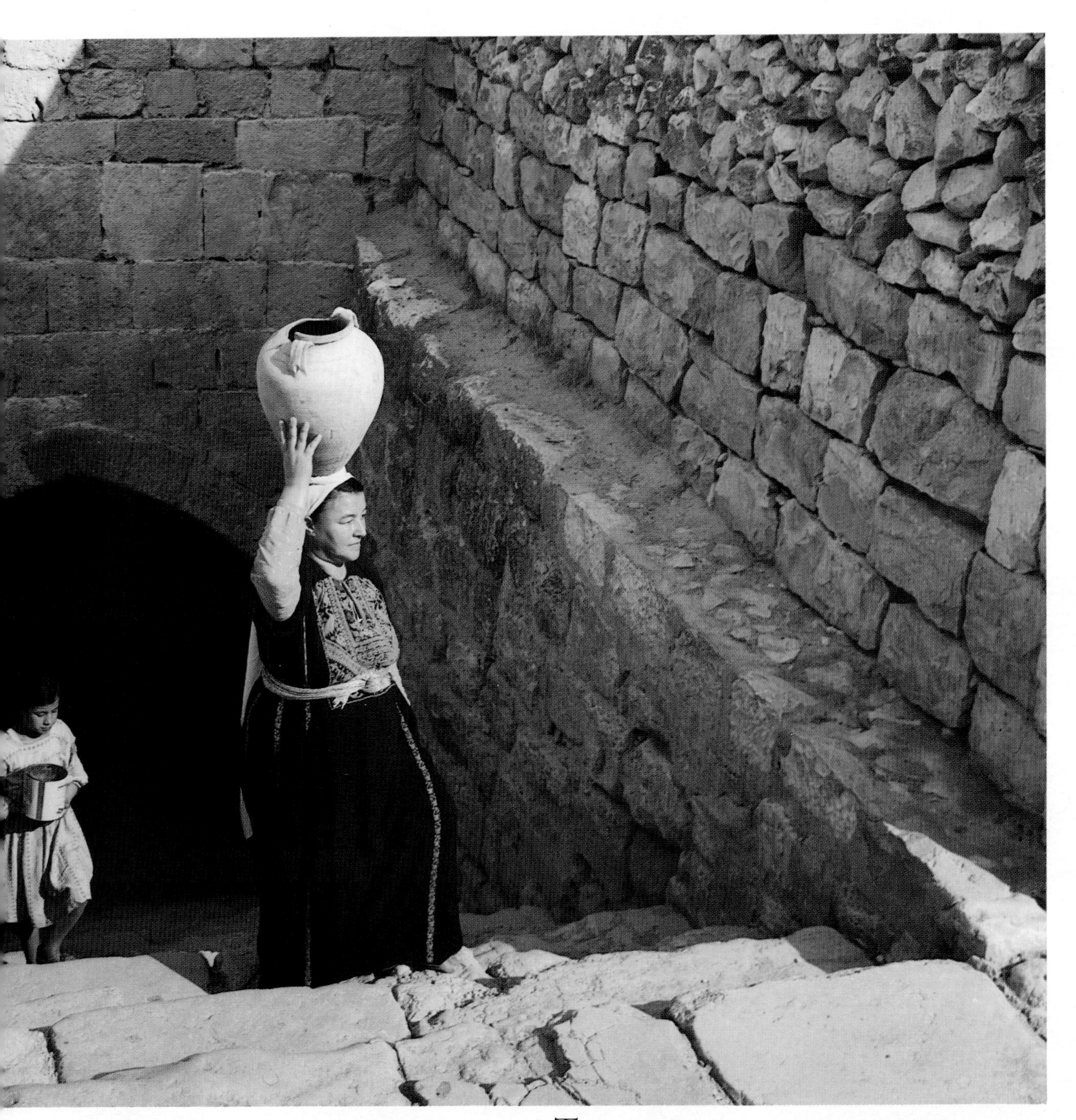

The POOL OF SILOAM dates from the reign of King Hezikiah and was built to supply water to the ancient city of Jerusalem. Its source is the Gihon spring, outside the city wall.

Surrounded on three sides by steep cliffs and mountains, the SEA OF GALILEE is subject to sudden changes in the weather. Cool winds coming down off the cliffs often stir up violent storms.

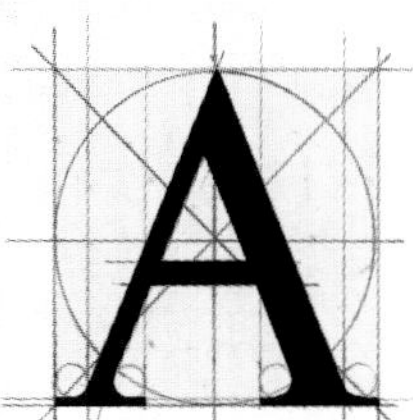

nd when even was come, the ship was in the midst of the sea, and he alone on the land.
And he saw them toiling in rowing;
for the wind was contrary unto them:
and about the fourth watch of the night
he cometh unto them,
walking upon the sea,
and would have passed by them.
But when they saw him
walking upon the sea,
they supposed it had been a spirit,
and cried out:
For they all saw him,
and were troubled.
And immediately he talked with them,
and saith unto them,
Be of good cheer: it is I;
be not afraid.

MARK 6: 47-50

Now a certain man was sick, named Lazarus, of Bethany, the town of Mary and her sister Martha. Therefore his sisters sent unto him saying, Lord, behold, he whom thou lovest is sick. Then said Jesus unto them plainly, Lazarus is dead. Then said Martha unto Jesus, Lord, if thou hadst been here, my brother had not died. But I know, that even now, whatsoever thou wilt ask of God, God will give it thee. Jesus saith unto her. . . . I am the resurrection, and the life: he that believeth in me, though he were dead, yet shall he live: and whosoever liveth and believeth in me shall never die.

Then they took away the stone from the place where the dead was laid. And Jesus lifted up his eyes, and said, Father, I thank thee that thou hast heard me. . . . And when he thus had spoken, he cried with a loud voice, Lazarus, come forth. And he that was dead came forth. . . .

JOHN 11: 1, 3, 14, 21-23, 25, 26, 41, 43, 44

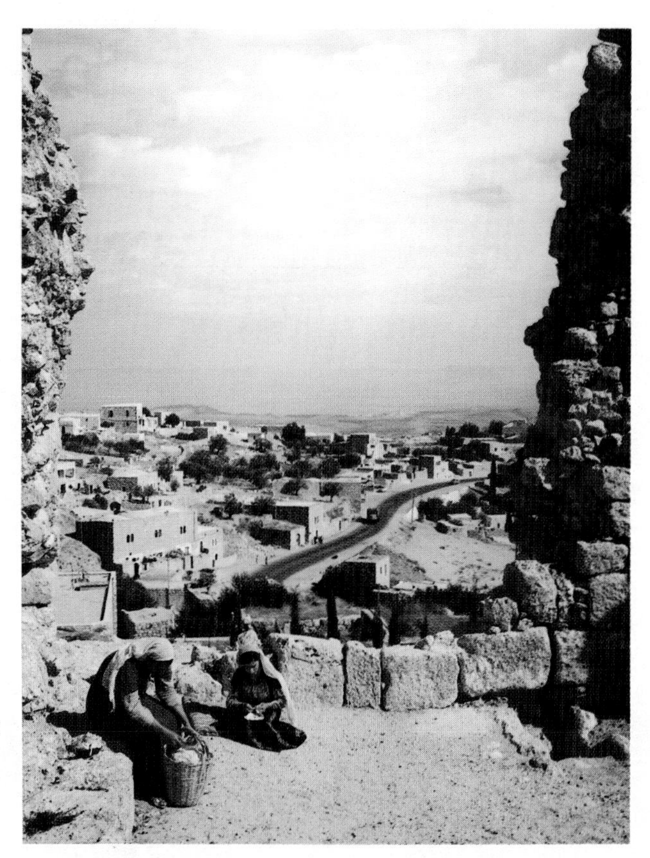

Just east of Jerusalem, on the slopes of the Mount of Olives, the village of BETHANY was the home of Mary, Martha, and Lazarus.

Believed by some to be the site of Lazarus' burial, this ANCIENT TOMB is near Bethany. Jesus' raising of Lazarus from the dead caused a stir among the religious authorities in Jerusalem.

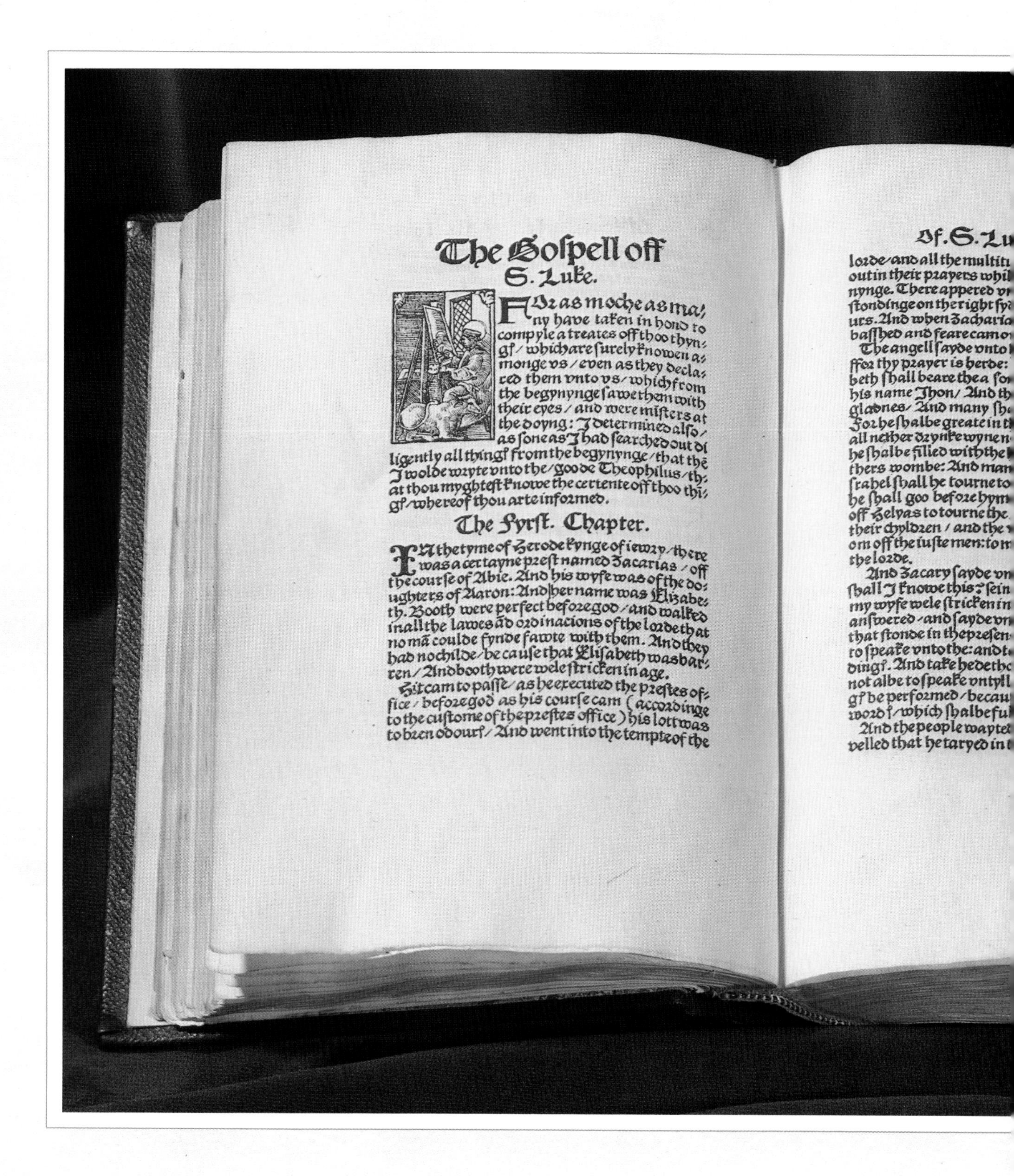

The Gospell off
S. Luke.

For as moche as many have taken in hond to compyle a treates off thoo thyngs / which are surely knowen amonge vs / even as they declared them vnto vs / which from the begynnynge sawe them with their eyes / and were misters at the doyng: I determined also / as sone as I had searched out diligently all thingſ from the begynnynge / that thē I wolde wryte vnto the / goode Theophilus / that thou myghtest knowe the certente off thoo thingſ / whereof thou arte informed.

The Fyrst. Chapter.

In the tyme of Herode kynge of iewry / there was a certayne prest named Zacarias / off the course of Abie. And his wyfe was of the doughters of Aaron: And her name was Elizabeth. Booth were perfect before god / and walked in all the lawes ād ordinacions of the lorde that no mā coulde fynde fawte with them. And they had no childe / be cause that Elisabeth was barren / And booth were wele stricken in age.

Hit cam to passe / as he executed the prestes office / before god as his course cam (accordinge to the custome of the prestes office) his lott was to bren odours / And went into the temple of the

Of. S. Lu

lorde / and all the multit
out in their prayers whil
nynge. There appered v
stondinge on the right sy
urs. And when Zacharia
basshed and feare cam o
The angell sayde vnto
ffor thy prayer is herde:
beth shall beare the a so
his name Jhon / And th
gladnes / And many sh
For he shalbe greate in t
all nether drynke wyne n
he shalbe filled with the
thers wombe: And man
Srahel shall he tourne to
he shall goo before hym
off Helyas to tourne the
their chyldren / and the
om off the iuste men: to m
the lorde.
And Zacary sayde vn
shall I knowe this? sein
my wyfe wele stricken in
answered / and sayde vn
that stonde in the presen
to speake vnto the: and t
dingſ. And take hede th
not albe to speake vntyll
gſ be performed / becau
wordſ / which shalbe ful
And the people wayte
velled that he taryed in t

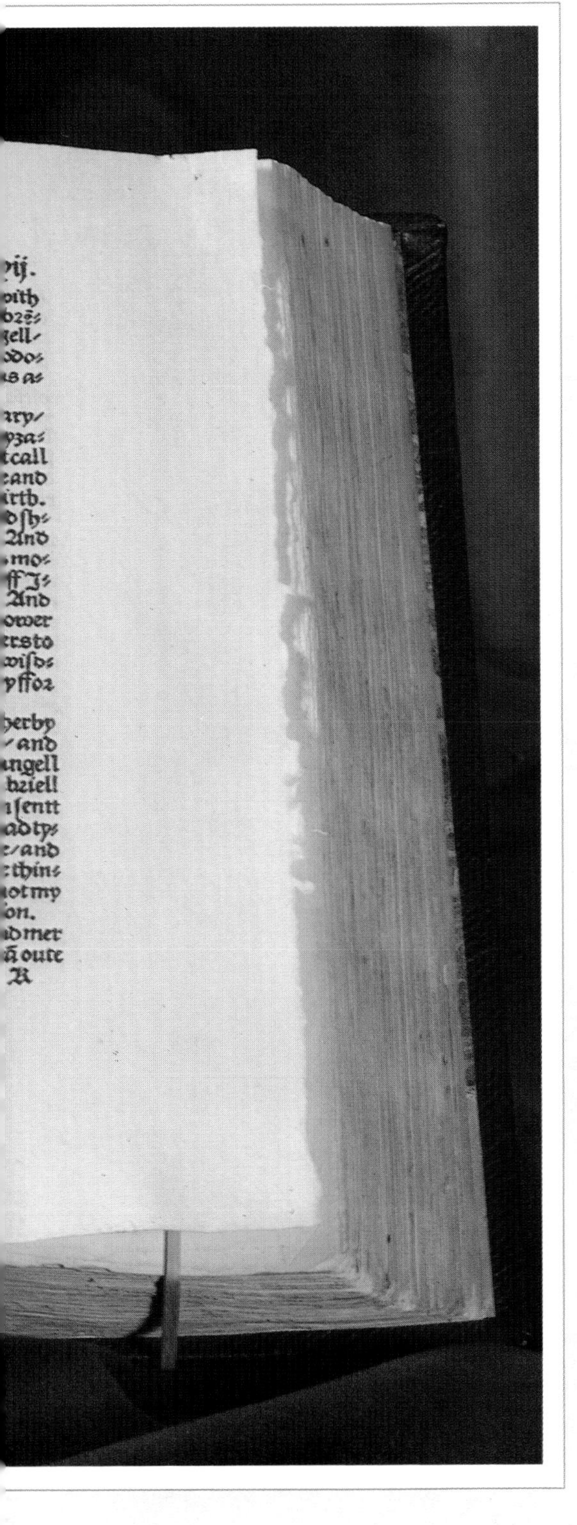

The Road to the Cross

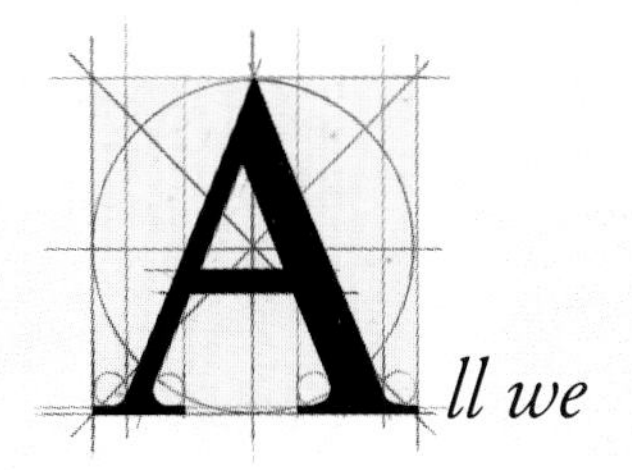

ll we

like sheep have gone astray;

we have turned every one

to his own way;

and the LORD hath laid on him

the iniquity of us all.

Isaiah 53: 6

In 1525, English reformer William Tyndale produced the first printed English translation of the Bible, translating first the New Testament and then part of the Old Testament from Greek. His Bible sold well in England, although it was officially banned by the Church of England. The TYNDALE BIBLE had great influence on the style of future Bible translation, including the King James Version. Because the Church opposed an unofficial translation of the Bible, William Tyndale was labeled a heretic and was burned at the stake in 1536. The Bible pictured dates from 1535.

And after six
days Jesus taketh with him Peter, and James,
and John, and leadeth them up into an
high mountain apart by themselves:
and he was transfigured before them.
And his raiment became shining,
exceeding white as snow;
so as no fuller on earth can white them.
And there was a cloud that overshadowed them:
and a voice came out of the cloud, saying,
This is my beloved Son: hear him.
And suddenly, when they had looked round
about, they saw no man any more,
save Jesus only with themselves. And as they
came down from the mountain, he charged
them that they should tell no man
what things they had seen, till the Son of man
were risen from the dead.
And they kept that saying with themselves,
questioning one with another what
the rising from the dead should mean.

MARK 9: 2-3, 7-10

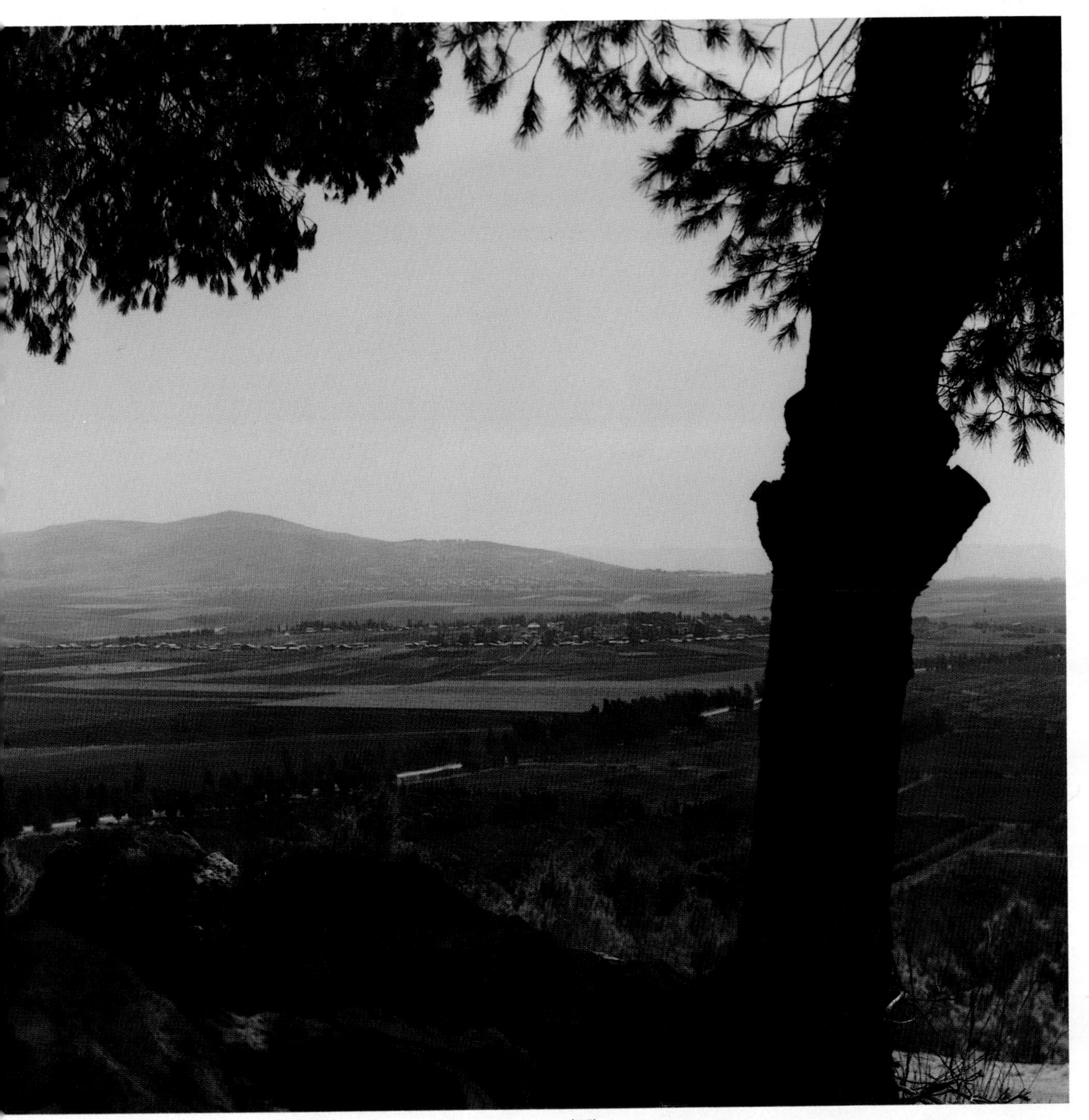

The VALLEY OF JEZREEL (also known as the Plain of Esdraelon) lies along the ancient border of Galilee and Samaria, a strategic military location as well as the convergence of two ancient trade routes. The valley was the site of many battles, including the battle of Megiddo. The Greek name for the valley is Armageddon.

A YOUNG BOY stands watch with his donkey colt just outside Capernaum near what is believed by many to be the site of the Sermon on the Mount.

And when they drew nigh unto Jerusalem, and were come to Bethphage, unto the mount of Olives, then sent Jesus two disciples, Saying unto them, Go into the village over against you, and straightway ye shall find an ass tied, and a colt with her: loose them, and bring them unto me. And if any man say ought unto you, ye shall say, The Lord hath need of them; and straightway he will send them.

All this was done, that it might be fulfilled which was spoken by the prophet, saying, Tell ye the daughter of Sion, Behold, thy King cometh unto thee, meek, and sitting upon an ass, and a colt the foal of an ass. And the disciples went, and did as Jesus commanded them, And brought the ass, and the colt, and put on them their clothes, and they set him thereon.

MATTHEW 21: 1-7

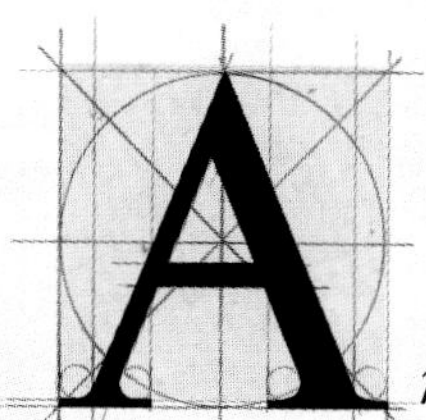

*nd a very
great multitude spread their garments
in the way; others cut down branches
from the trees, and strawed
them in the way.
And the multitudes that went before,
and that followed, cried, saying,
Hosanna to the son of David:
Blessed is he that cometh
in the name of the Lord;
Hosanna in the highest.*

*And when he was come into Jerusalem,
all the city was moved, saying,
Who is this?
And the multitude said,
This is Jesus
the prophet of Nazareth
of Galilee.*

MATTHEW 21: 8-11

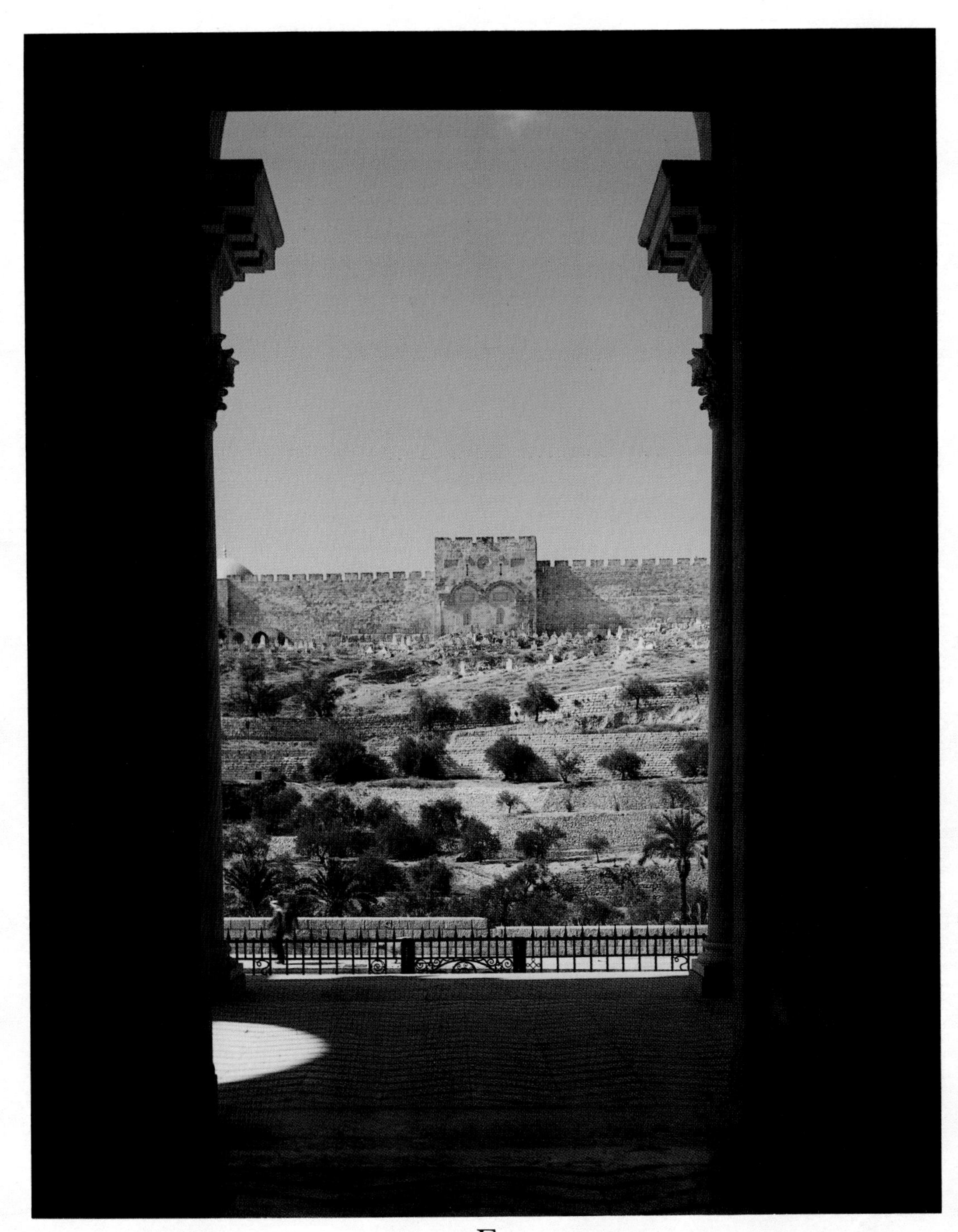

Even though it has been walled over for centuries, the GOLDEN GATE, one of the many entrances into the walled city of Jerusalem, is believed to be where Jesus made His triumphant entry into the city. Some Bible scholars believe that Jesus will return through this gate.

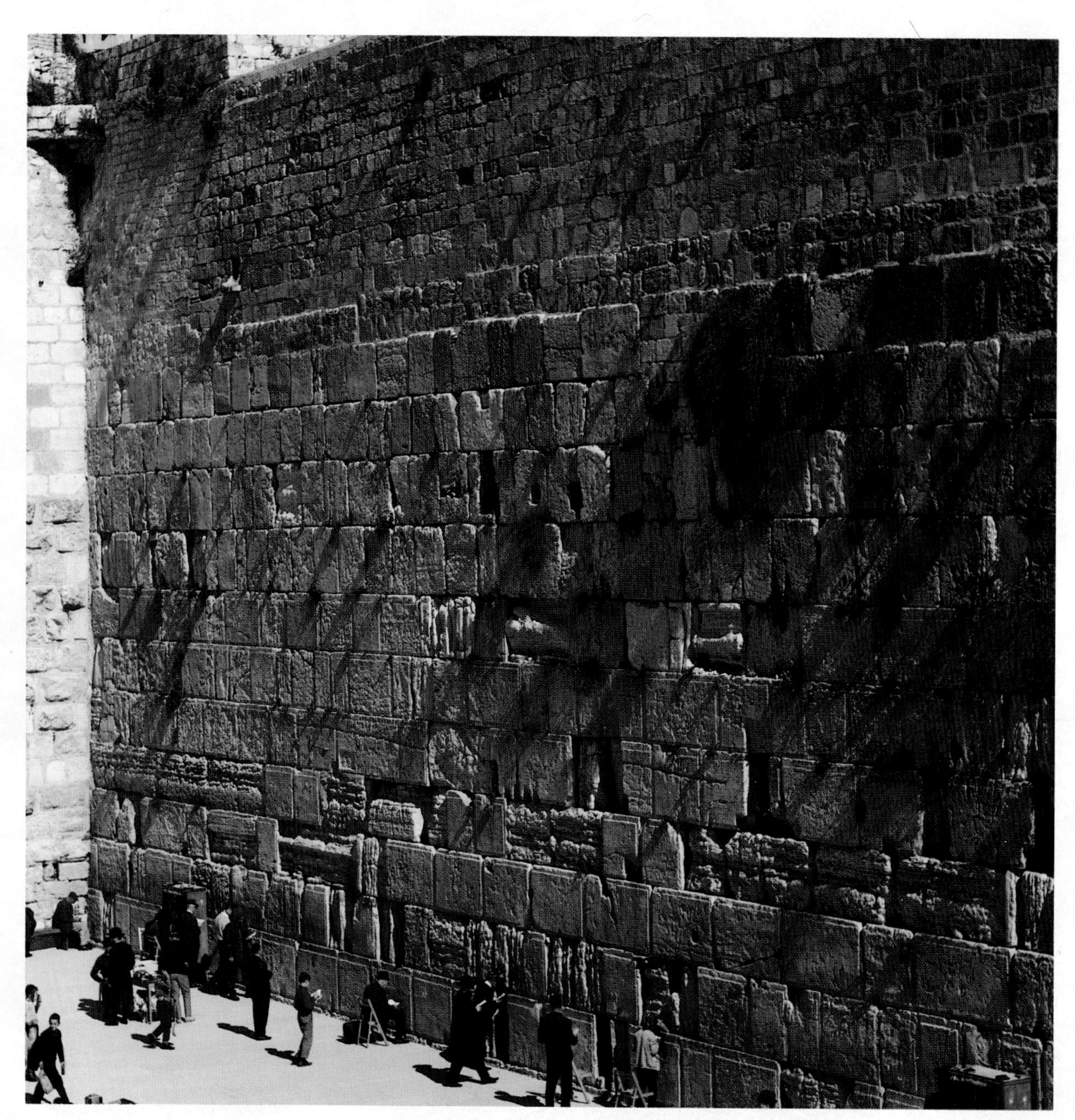

The WESTERN or "WAILING" WALL, all that remains of Herod's temple, is a sacred place of prayer for the Jewish people. The massive stones (averaging three to four feet high and four to ten feet long and weighing as much as two tons) were cut and chiseled so perfectly that no mortar was needed. Built over the site of Solomon's temple, Herod's temple was even grander than the first.

And Jesus went into the temple of God, and cast out all them that sold and bought in the temple, and overthrew the tables of the moneychangers . . . And said unto them, It is written, My house shall be called the house of prayer; but ye have made it a den of thieves.
And the blind and the lame came to him in the temple; and he healed them.

And when the chief priests and scribes saw the wonderful things that he did, and the children crying in the temple, and saying, Hosanna to the son of David; they were sore displeased, And said unto him, Hearest thou what these say?
And Jesus saith unto them, Yea; have ye never read, Out of the mouth of babes and sucklings thou hast perfected praise?
And he left them, and went out of the city into Bethany; and he lodged there.

MATTHEW 21: 12-17

And Jesus went out, and. . . . said unto them . . . There shall not be left here one stone upon another, that shall not be thrown down. And . . . the disciples came unto him privately, saying. . . . what shall be the sign of thy coming, and of the end of the world? And Jesus . . . said. . . . many shall come in my name, saying, I am Christ; and shall deceive many. And ye shall hear of wars and rumours of wars: see that ye be not troubled: for all these things must come to pass, but the end is not yet. For there shall arise false Christs, and false prophets. . . . And then shall appear the sign of the Son of man in heaven: and then shall all the tribes of the earth mourn, and they shall see the Son of man coming in the clouds of heaven with power and great glory. And he shall send his angels with a great sound of a trumpet, and they shall gather together his elect from the four winds, from one end of heaven to the other.

MATTHEW 24: 1-6, 24, 30, 31

Although JERUSALEM is not well located commercially—far inland from any major seaport—it has been inhabited since before the time of Abraham. The surrounding hills and valleys made it easy to defend and led to its establishment as the political and religious center of the country.

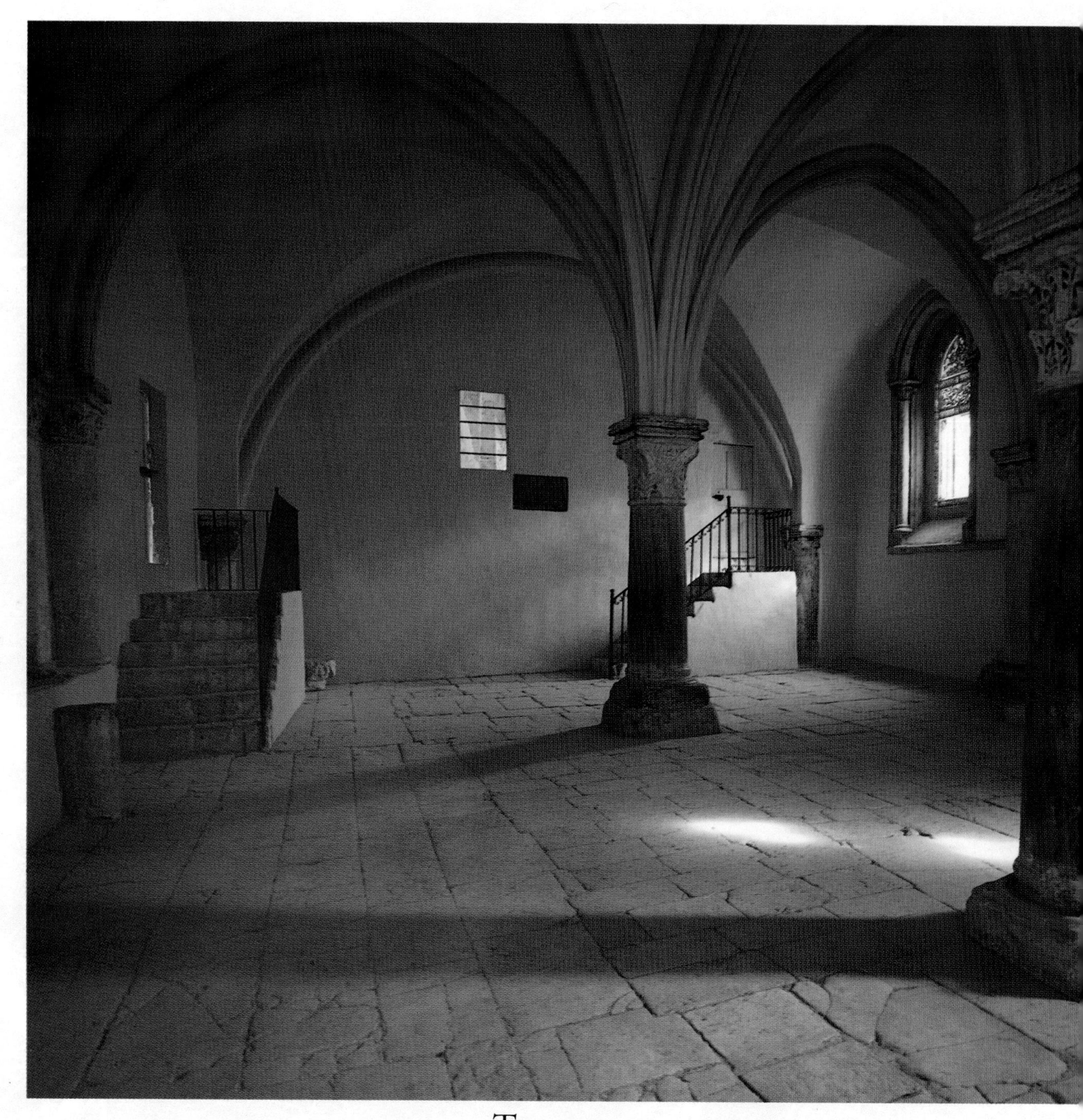

The actual location of the Last Supper is not known; but, after the Crusades, the Church of St. Mary of Zion was built on the traditional site of the UPPER ROOM. The room pictured, the Cenaculum, was set aside as a shrine to the event.

And the first day of unleavened bread, his disciples said unto him, Where wilt thou that we go and prepare that thou mayest eat the passover?
And he sendeth forth two of his disciples, and saith unto them, Go ye into the city, and there shall meet you a man bearing a pitcher of water: follow him.
And he will shew you a large upper room furnished and prepared: there make ready for us.

And as they did eat, Jesus took bread, and blessed, and brake it, and gave to them, and said, Take, eat: this is my body. And he took the cup, and when he had given thanks, he gave it to them: and they all drank of it.
And he said unto them, This is my blood of the new testament, which is shed for many.
And when they had sung an hymn, they went out into the mount of Olives.

MARK 14: 12, 13, 15, 22-24, 26

*And they came
to a place which was named Gethsemane:
and he saith to his disciples,
Sit ye here, while I shall pray. . . .
My soul is exceeding sorrowful unto death:
tarry ye here, and watch.*

*And he went forward a little, and fell on the
ground, and prayed that, if it were possible,
the hour might pass from him.
And he said, Abba, Father,
all things are possible unto thee;
take away this cup from me: nevertheless
not what I will, but what thou wilt.*

*. . . the hour is come;
behold, the Son of man
is betrayed into the hands of sinners.
Rise up, let us go;
lo, he that betrayeth me is at hand.*

MARK 14: 32, 34-36, 41, 42

Although THE GARDEN OF GETHSEMANE (meaning "olive press") is known to have been on the Mount of Olives, located east of Jerusalem and the temple, scholars disagree on its exact location. Pictured here is one traditional site. These olive trees may date from the time of Christ or before since olive trees grow very slowly and propagate by sending out shoots from their roots.

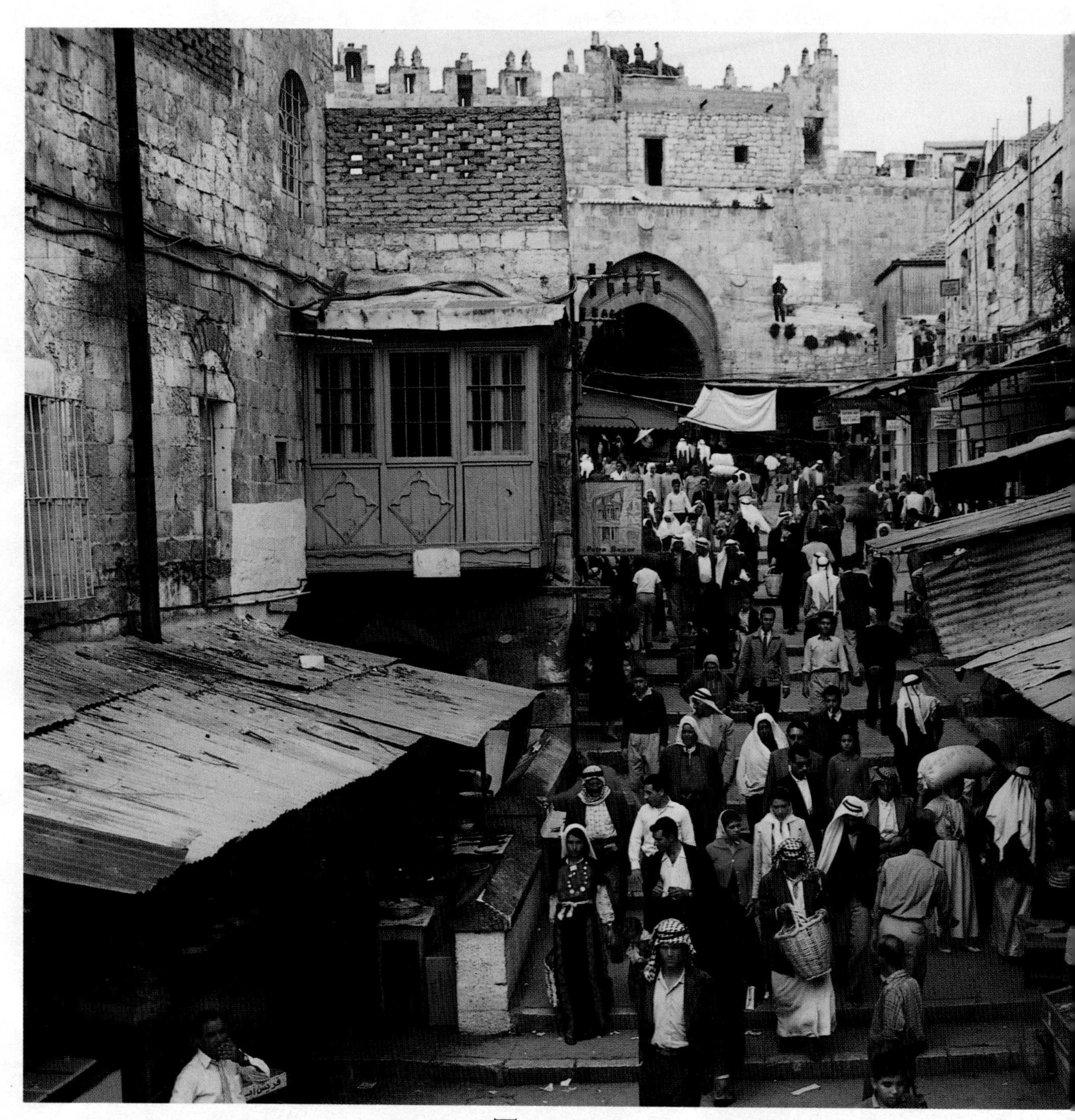

The streets of the old city in JERUSALEM have changed little over the centuries. Today, these ancient, narrow streets look much as they did when Christ walked here.

And they that had laid hold on Jesus led him away to Caiaphas the high priest. . . . But Peter followed him afar off . . . and went in . . . to see the end. Now the chief priests, and elders, and all the council, sought false witness against Jesus. . . . But found none. . . . At the last came two false witnesses, And said, This fellow said, I am able to destroy the temple of God, and to build it in three days. And the high priest arose, and said unto him, Answerest thou nothing? . . . But Jesus held his peace. And the high priest . . . said . . . tell us whether thou be the Christ, the Son of God. Jesus saith unto him, Thou hast said: nevertheless I say unto you, Hereafter shall ye see the Son of man sitting on the right hand of power, and coming in the clouds of heaven. Then the high priest rent his clothes, saying, He hath spoke blasphemy. . . . What think ye? They answered and said, He is guilty of death.

MATTHEW 26: 57-66

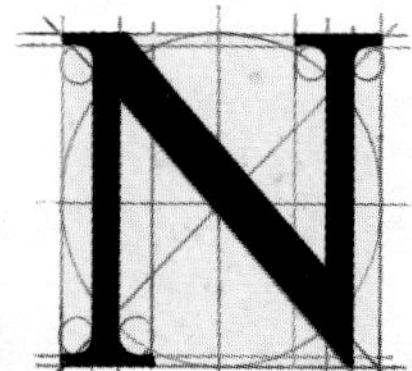

ow Peter sat without in the palace: and a damsel came unto him, saying, Thou also wast with Jesus of Galilee. But he denied before them all, saying, I know not what thou sayest. And when he was gone out into the porch, another maid saw him, and said unto them that were there, This fellow was also with Jesus of Nazareth. And again he denied with an oath, I do not know the man.

And after a while came unto him they that stood by, and said to Peter, Surely thou also art one of them; for thy speech bewrayeth thee. Then began he to curse and to swear, saying, I know not the man. And immediately the cock crew. And Peter remembered the word of Jesus, which said unto him, Before the cock crow, thou shalt deny me thrice. And he went out, and wept bitterly.

MATTHEW 26: 69-75

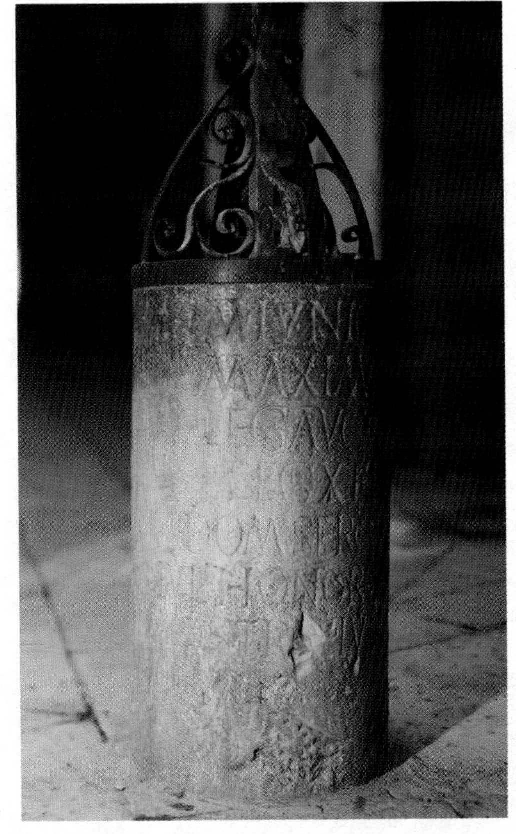

This ROMAN 10TH LEGION STONE MARKER is one of many which, at the time of Christ, were scattered throughout Jerusalem as reminders of the occupational force. Today only a few remain.

These ROMAN AQUEDUCTS AT CAESAREA are examples of Roman construction under Pontius Pilate. The Emperor Tiberius ordered Pilate to stand trial for the execution of Samarians in A.D. 37, but the emperor's death meant a reprieve for Pilate. Except for the trial of Christ, Pilate is a minor governor in Roman history.

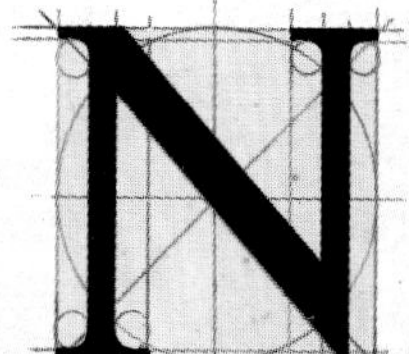

*ow at that
feast the governor was wont to release unto the
people a prisoner, whom they would.
And they had then a notable prisoner,
called Barabbas. . . . Pilate said unto them,
Whom will ye that I release unto you?
Barabbas, or Jesus which is called Christ?
They said, Barabbas. Pilate saith unto them,
What shall I do then with
Jesus which is called Christ?
They all say unto him, Let him be crucified.
And the governor said, Why, what evil hath he
done? But they cried out the more, saying,
Let him be crucified.*

*When Pilate saw that he could prevail nothing,
but that rather a tumult was made,
he took water, and washed his hands
before the multitude, saying, I am innocent of
the blood of this just person:
see ye to it.*

MATTHEW 27: 15-17, 21-24

The PONTIUS PILATE STONE, discovered by Italian archaeologists in 1961, is the governor's only known inscription. It dedicates the theater at Caesarea to the honor of the Roman Emperor Tiberius.

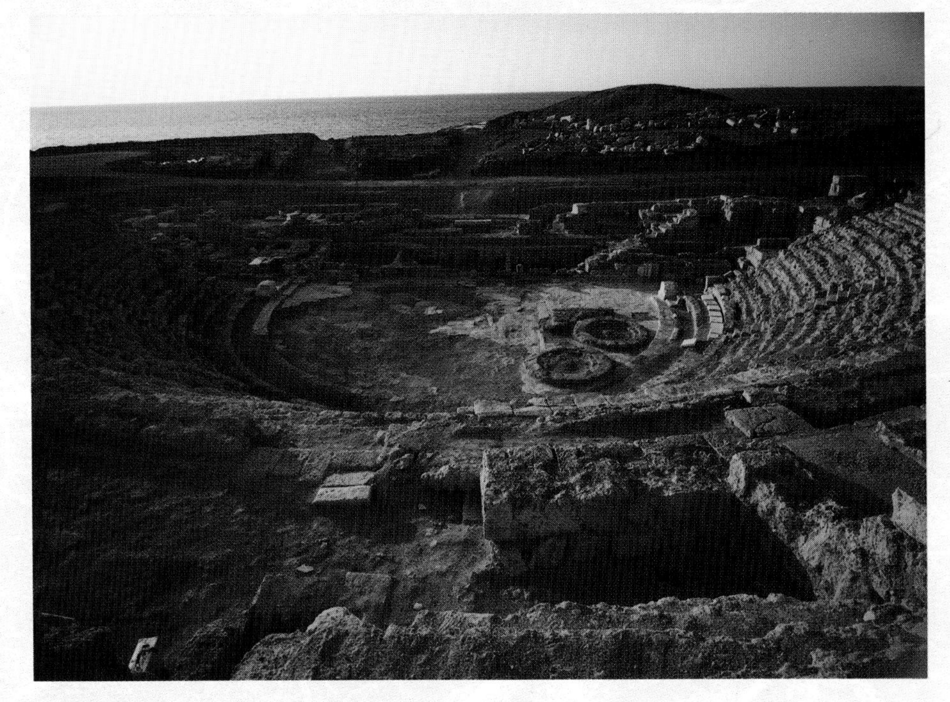

The Pontius Pilate Stone was found here at this ancient AMPHITHEATER in CAESAREA. Scholars believe Pilate often attended festivals at this once magnificent site.

*Then the soldiers
of the governor took Jesus into the common
hall, and gathered unto him
the whole band of soldiers.
And they stripped him,
and put on him a scarlet robe.*

*And when they had platted
a crown of thorns, they put it
upon his head, and a reed
in his right hand:
and they bowed the knee
before him, and mocked him, saying,
Hail, King of the Jews!
And they spit upon him, and took the reed,
and smote him on the head.*

*And after that they had mocked him,
they took the robe off from him,
and put his own raiment on him,
and led him away to crucify him.*

MATTHEW 27: 27-31

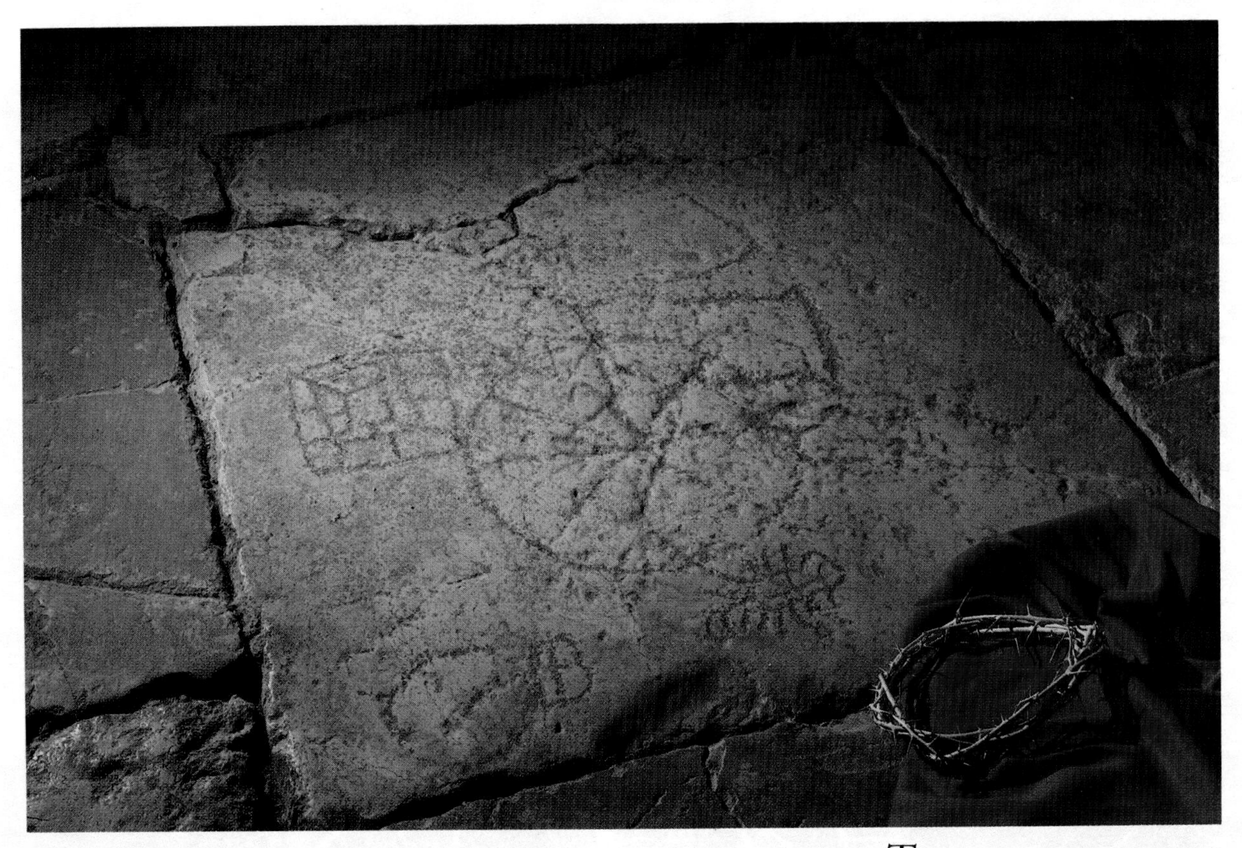

These WORDS AND GAMES scratched into the stone floor in the courtyard area of Herod's Temple could have been made by Roman guards while standing watch over Jesus. Some of the games are similar to our ticktacktoe.

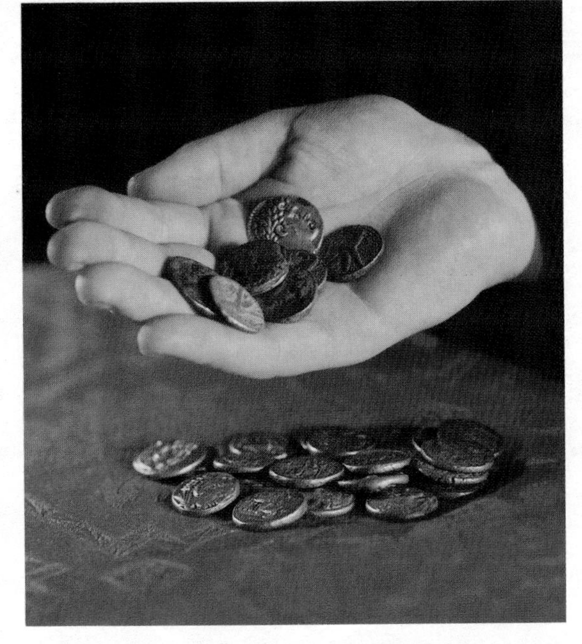

The bribe that Judas received to betray Jesus to the authorities, THIRTY PIECES OF SILVER, was not a lot of money and it is not known why he accepted it to turn traitor. The coins pictured are authentic Roman silver coins from the time of Jesus and are in the collection of the Franciscan Museum inside the walls of the Old City of Jerusalem.

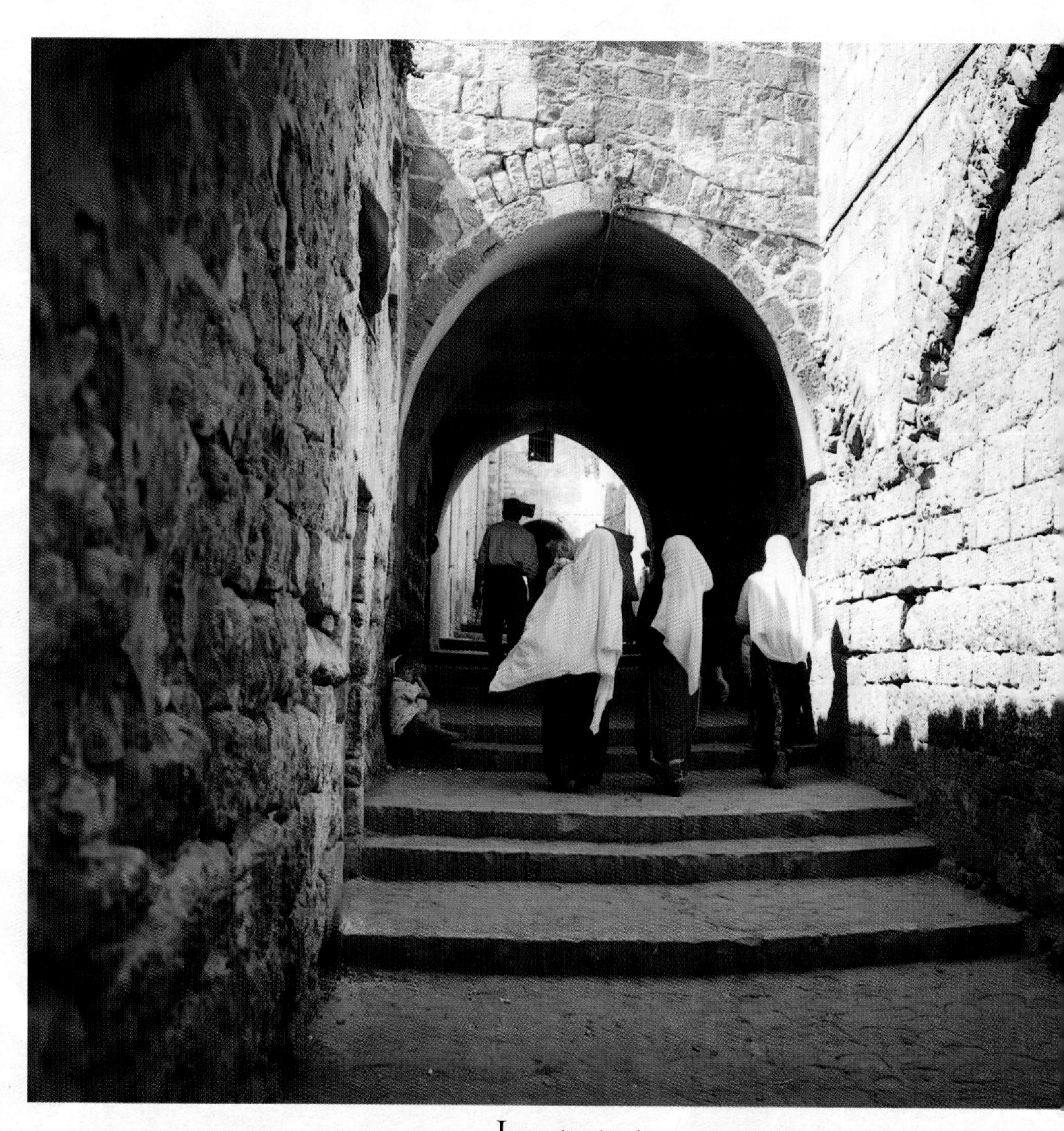

Immediately after Jesus' trial, He was sentenced. He bore His cross through the streets of Jerusalem until he collapsed and the burden of the cross was handed over to Simon of Cyrene. The VIA DOLOROSA, or the Way of the Cross, has changed little throughout the centuries.

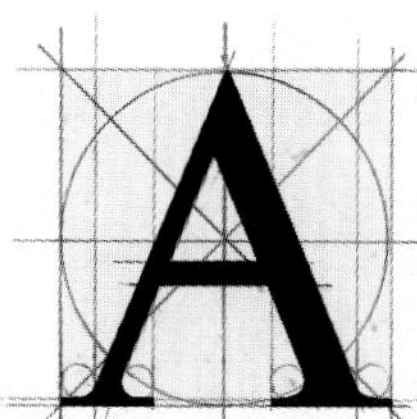

And as they
led him away, they laid hold upon one
Simon, a Cyrenian, coming out of the country,
and on him they laid the cross,
that he might bear it after Jesus.
And there followed him
a great company of people. . . .
which also bewailed and lamented him.

But Jesus turning unto them said,
Daughters of Jerusalem, weep not for me,
but weep for yourselves, and for your children.
For, behold, the days are coming,
in the which they shall say,
Blessed are the barren. . . .
Then shall they begin to say
to the mountains,
Fall on us; and to the hills, Cover us.
For if they do these things in a green tree,
what shall be done in the dry?

LUKE 23: 26-31

And they bring him unto the place Golgotha, which is, being interpreted, The place of a skull. And when they had crucified him, they parted his garments, casting lots upon them, what every man should take. And it was the third hour. . . . And with him they crucify two thieves; the one on his right hand, and the other on his left. And the scripture was fulfilled, which saith, And he was numbered with the transgressors. And at the ninth hour Jesus cried with a loud voice, saying. . . . My God, my God, why hast thou forsaken me? And Jesus cried with a loud voice, and gave up the ghost. And the veil of the temple was rent in twain. . . . And when the centurion, which stood over against him, saw that he so cried out, and gave up the ghost, he said, Truly this man was the Son of God.

MARK 15: 22, 24, 25, 27, 28, 34, 37-39

Bible scholars disagree on the exact location of Jesus' crucifixion, but most believe that GOLGOTHA (meaning "place of a skull") was at the top of these rugged cliffs, which resemble a skull.

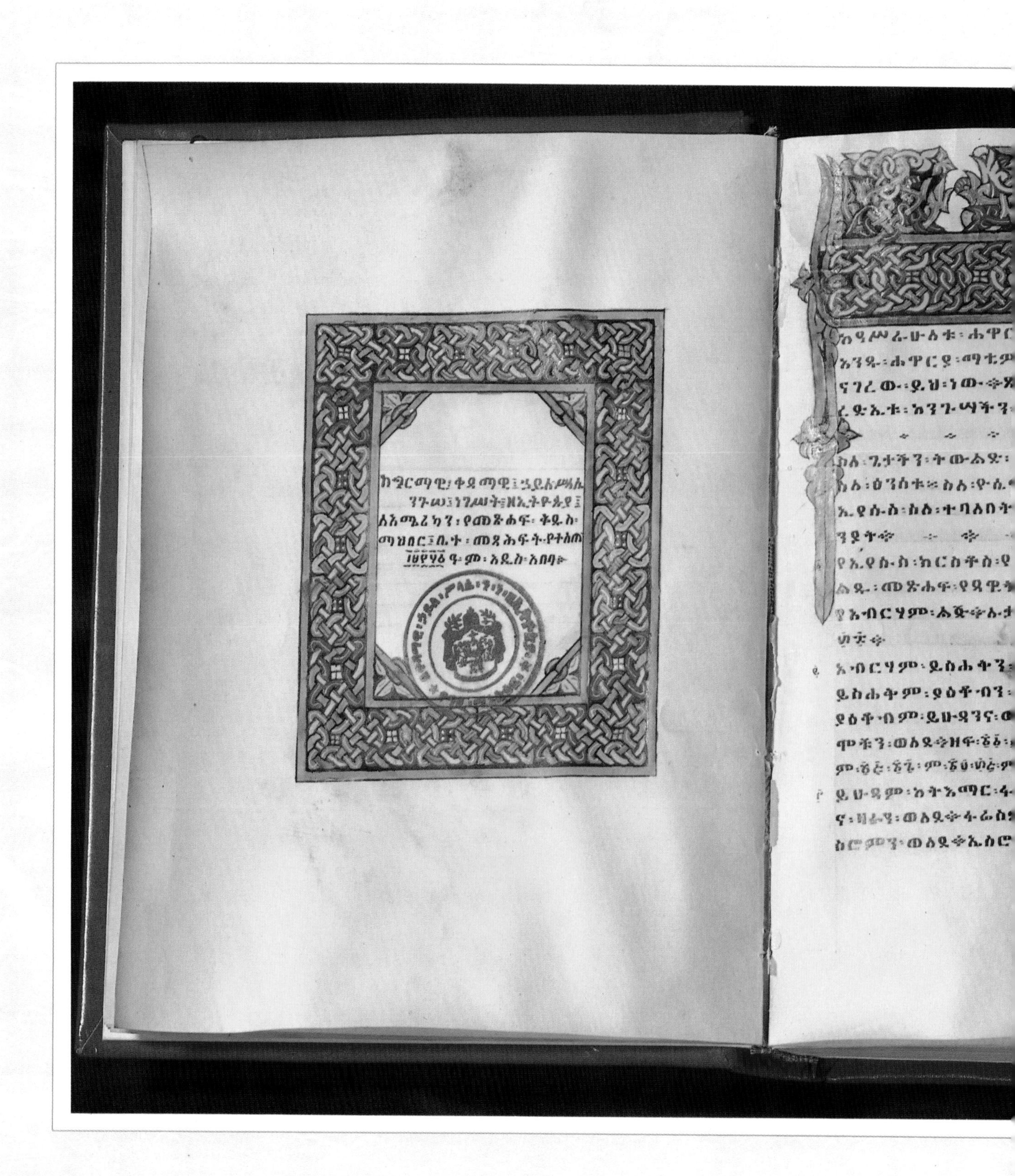

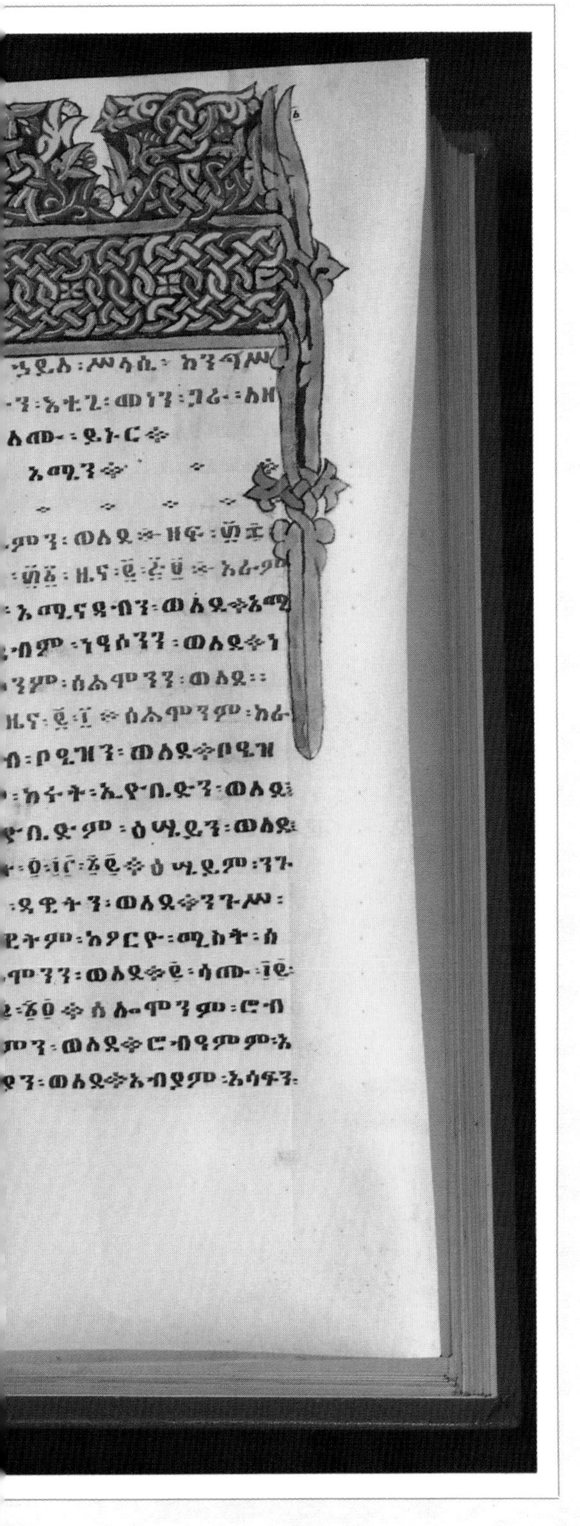

THE TRIUMPH

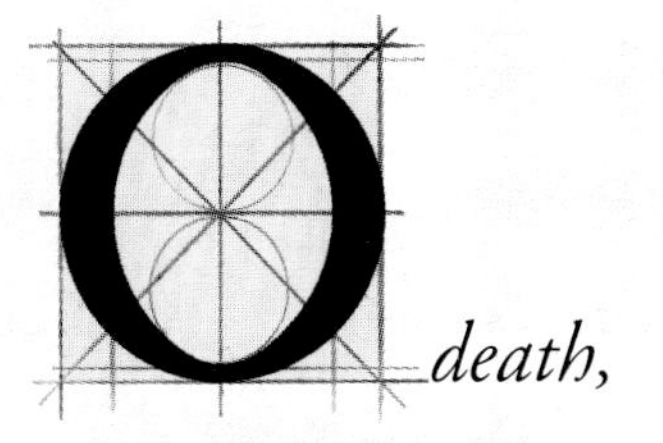

O death,

where is thy sting?

O grave, where is thy victory?

Thanks be to God,

which giveth us the victory

through our Lord Jesus Christ.

1 CORINTHIANS 15: 55-57

Over the centuries, with the spread of Christianity, the Bible has been translated into many different tongues and today is available in over 2,000 languages. The AMHARIC BIBLE pictured was printed in the state language of Ethiopia and bears the official seal of the Emperor Haile Selassie, the self-described "Lion of Judah" whose royal family claims descent from the Queen of Sheba and King Solomon.

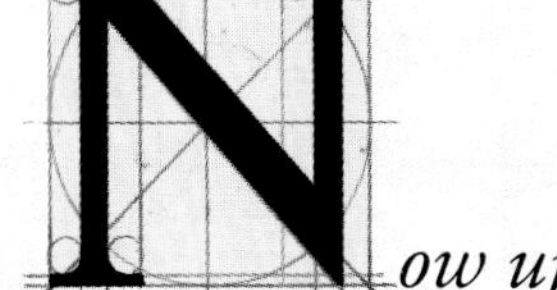*ow upon*
the first day of the week, very early in the
morning, they came unto the sepulchre,
bringing the spices which they had prepared,
and certain others with them.
And they found the stone rolled away from the
sepulchre. And they entered in, and found not
the body of the Lord Jesus.

And it came to pass, as they were much
perplexed thereabout, behold, two men
stood by them in shining garments:
And . . . said unto them,
Why seek ye the living among the dead?
He is not here, but is risen: remember how he
spake unto you when he was yet in Galilee,
Saying, the Son of man must be delivered into
the hands of sinful men, and be crucified,
and the third day rise again.
And they remembered his words . . .
and told all these things unto . . . the rest.

LUKE 24: 1-8

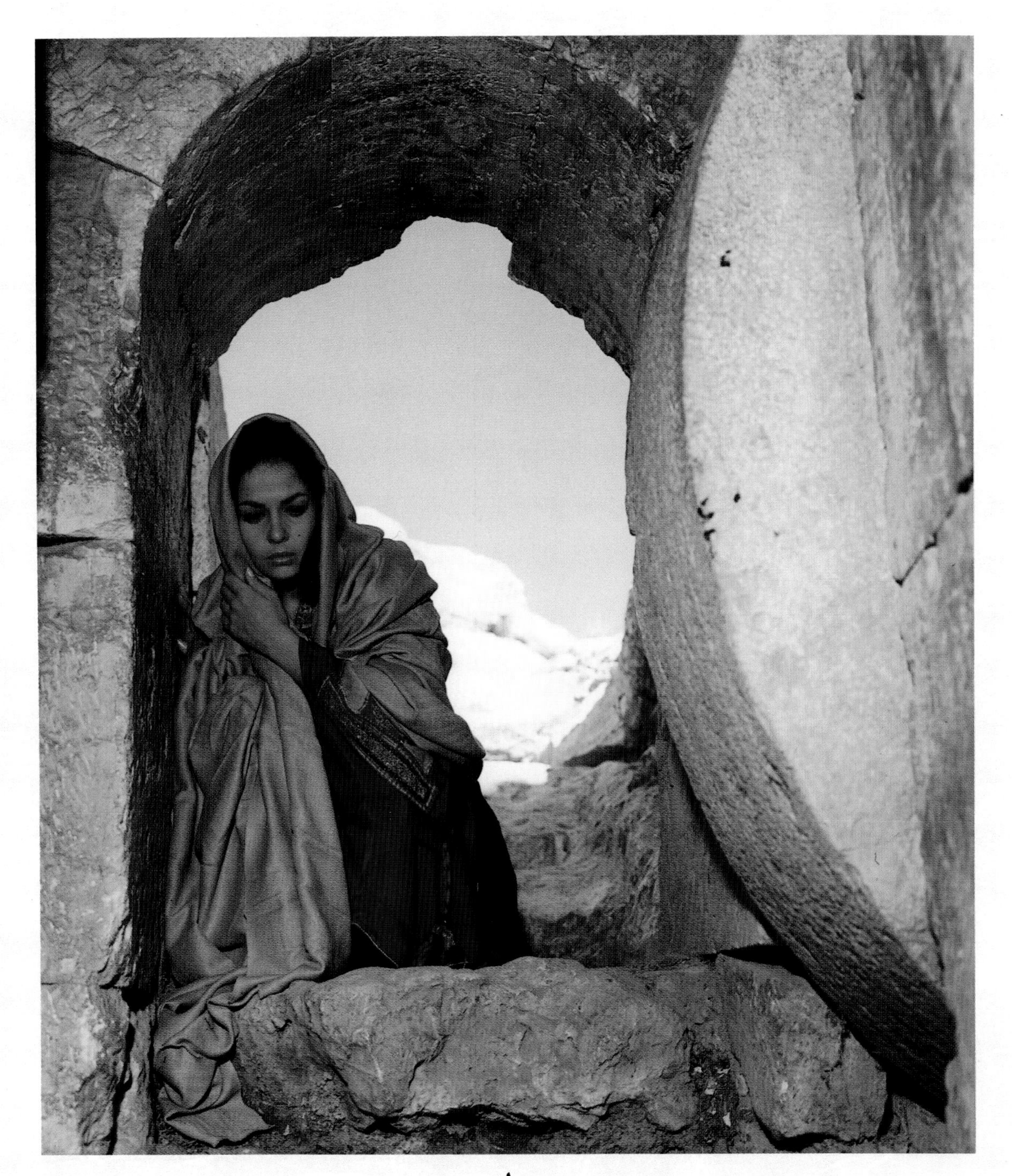

A woman in traditional costume poses at the entrance to a tomb that dates from the time of Christ's death. The massive rolling stone sealed the tomb so no one person could open it.

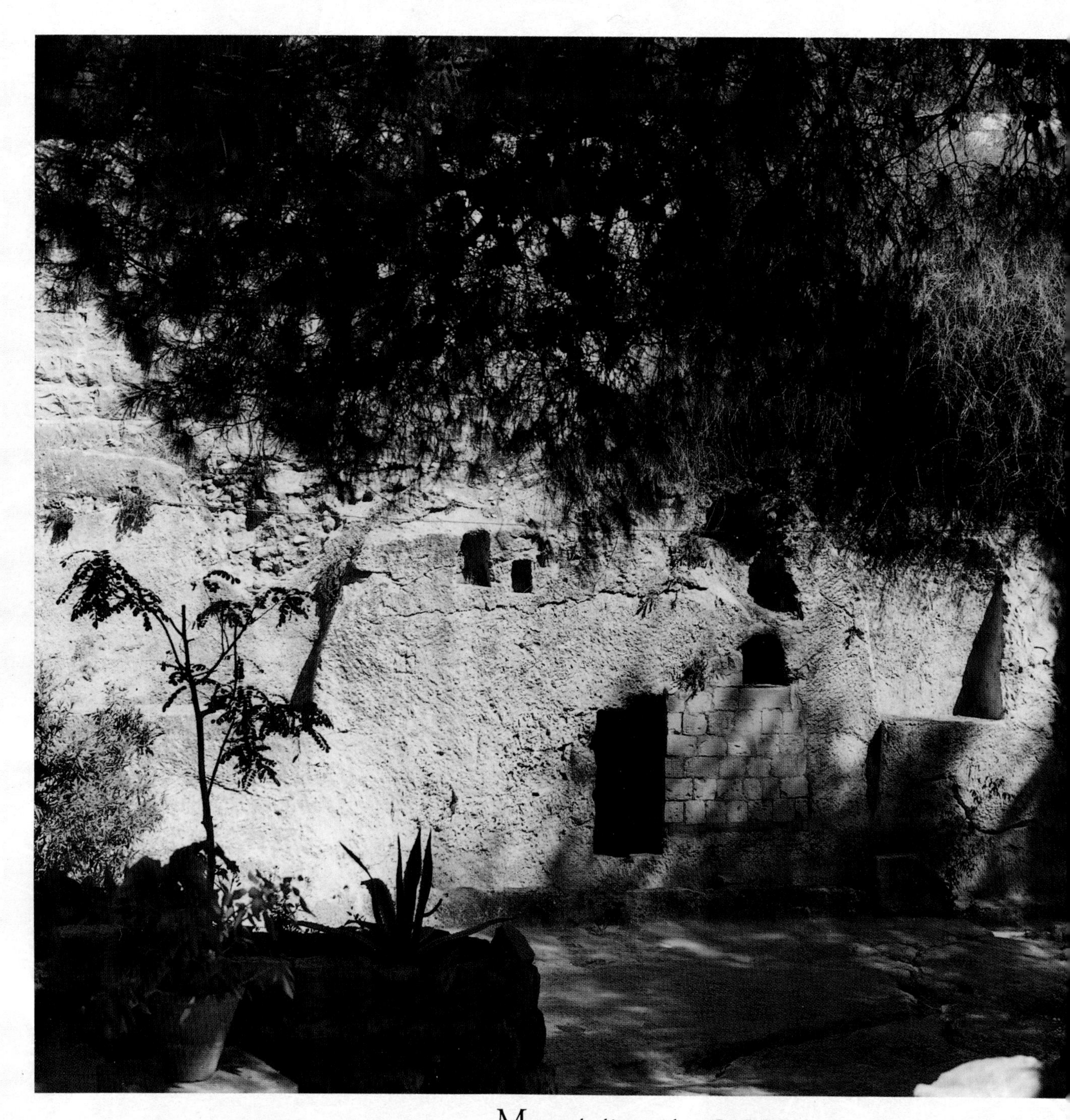

Many believe the GARDEN TOMB, in the peaceful surroundings of the Garden of Joseph of Arimathea, to be the tomb in which Christ was buried. The trough seen in front of the tomb was used to guide the massive rolling stone in place. Some scholars, however, believe that the tomb found by the Emperor Constantine's workers in A.D. 326—and now part of the Church of the Holy Sepulchre—might be the authentic one.

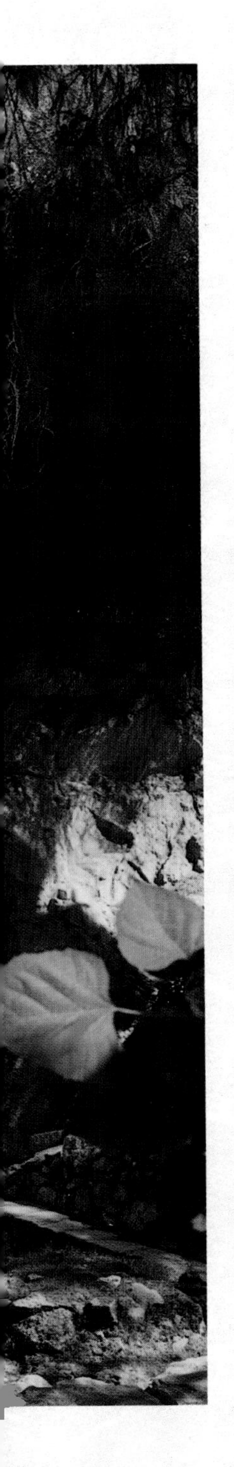

And, behold, two of them went that same day to a village called Emmaus. . . . And it came to pass, that . . . Jesus himself drew near. . . . But their eyes were holden that they should not know him. And he said unto them, What manner of communications are these that ye have one to another as ye walk, and are sad? And the one of them . . . said unto him, Art thou only a stranger . . . and hast not known the things which are come to pass. . . . concerning Jesus of Nazareth. . . . the chief priests and our rulers . . . have crucified him. Then he said unto them, O fools, and slow of heart to believe all that the prophets have spoken: Ought not Christ to have suffered these things, and to enter into his glory? And they drew nigh unto the village. . . . And it came to pass, as he sat at meat with them, he took bread, and blessed it. . . . And their eyes were opened, and they knew him; and he vanished out of their sight.

LUKE 24: 13, 15-20, 25, 26, 28-31

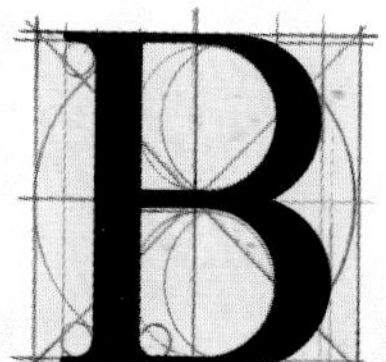

ut when the morning was now come, Jesus stood on the shore: but the disciples knew not that it was Jesus. Then Jesus saith unto them, Children, have ye any meat? They answered him, No. And he said unto them, Cast the net on the right side of the ship, and ye shall find. They cast therefore, and now they were not able to draw it for the multitude of fishes.

Therefore that diciple whom Jesus loved saith unto Peter, It is the Lord. Jesus saith unto them, Come and dine. And none of the disciples durst ask him, Who art thou? knowing that it was the Lord. This is now the third time that Jesus shewed himself to his disciples, after that he was risen from the dead.

JOHN 21: 4-7, 12, 14

Although often racked by violent storms brought on by the diverse surrounding landscape, the SEA OF GALILEE can be a calm and peaceful place, particularly in the early morning hours.

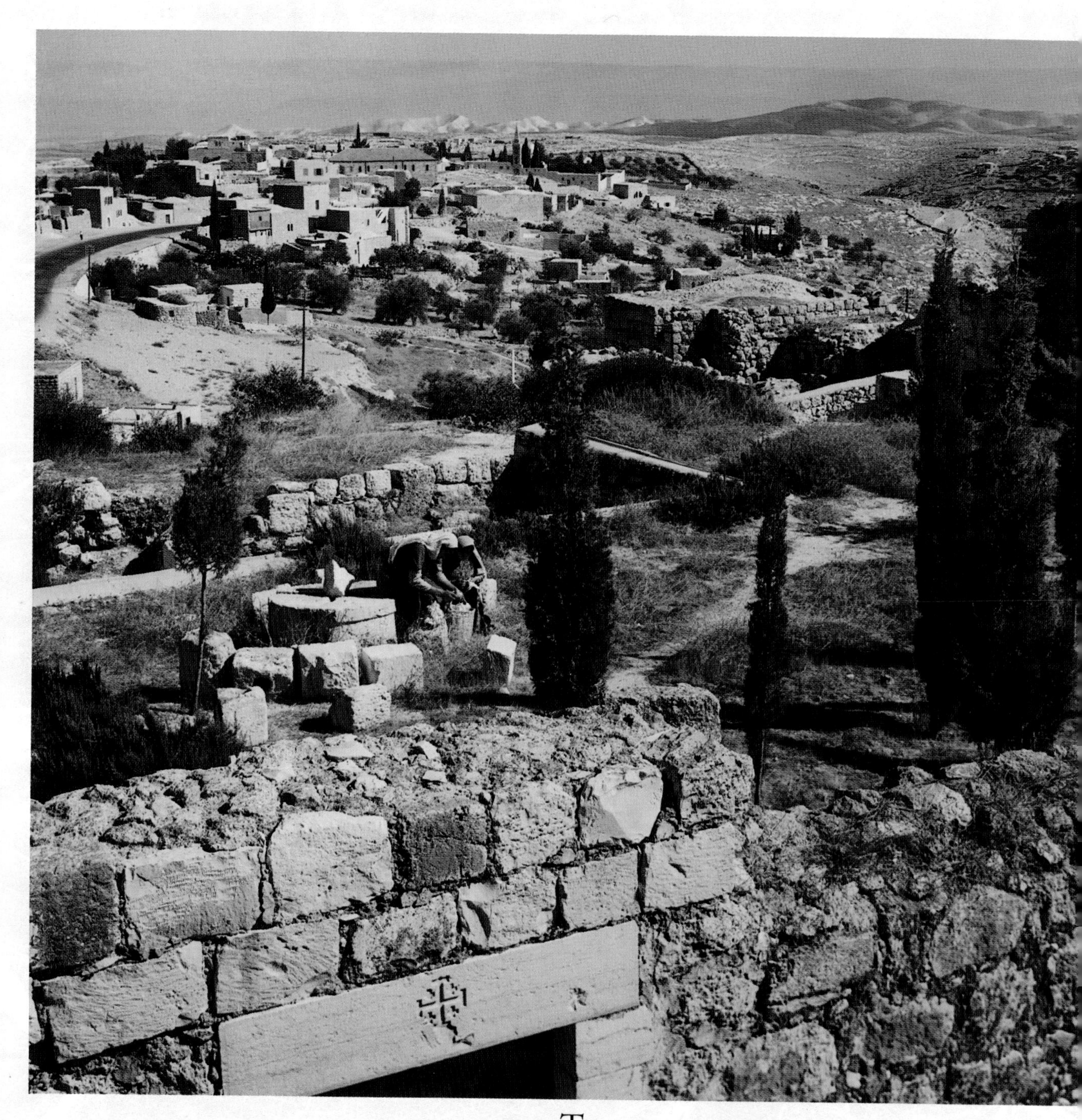

The village of BETHANY, between Jerusalem and Jericho, was the scene of many important events in Jesus' ministry. He spent at least one night in Bethany at the home of His friends, Mary, Martha, and Lazarus.

And he said unto them, These are the words which I spake unto you, while I was yet with you, that all things must be fulfilled, which were written in the law of Moses, and in the prophets, and in the psalms, concerning me. Then opened he their understanding, that they might understand the scriptures, And said unto them, Thus it is written, and thus it behoved Christ to suffer, and to rise from the dead the third day: And ye are witnesses of these things.

And he led them out as far as to Bethany, and he lifted up his hands, and blessed them.

LUKE 24: 44-46, 48, 50

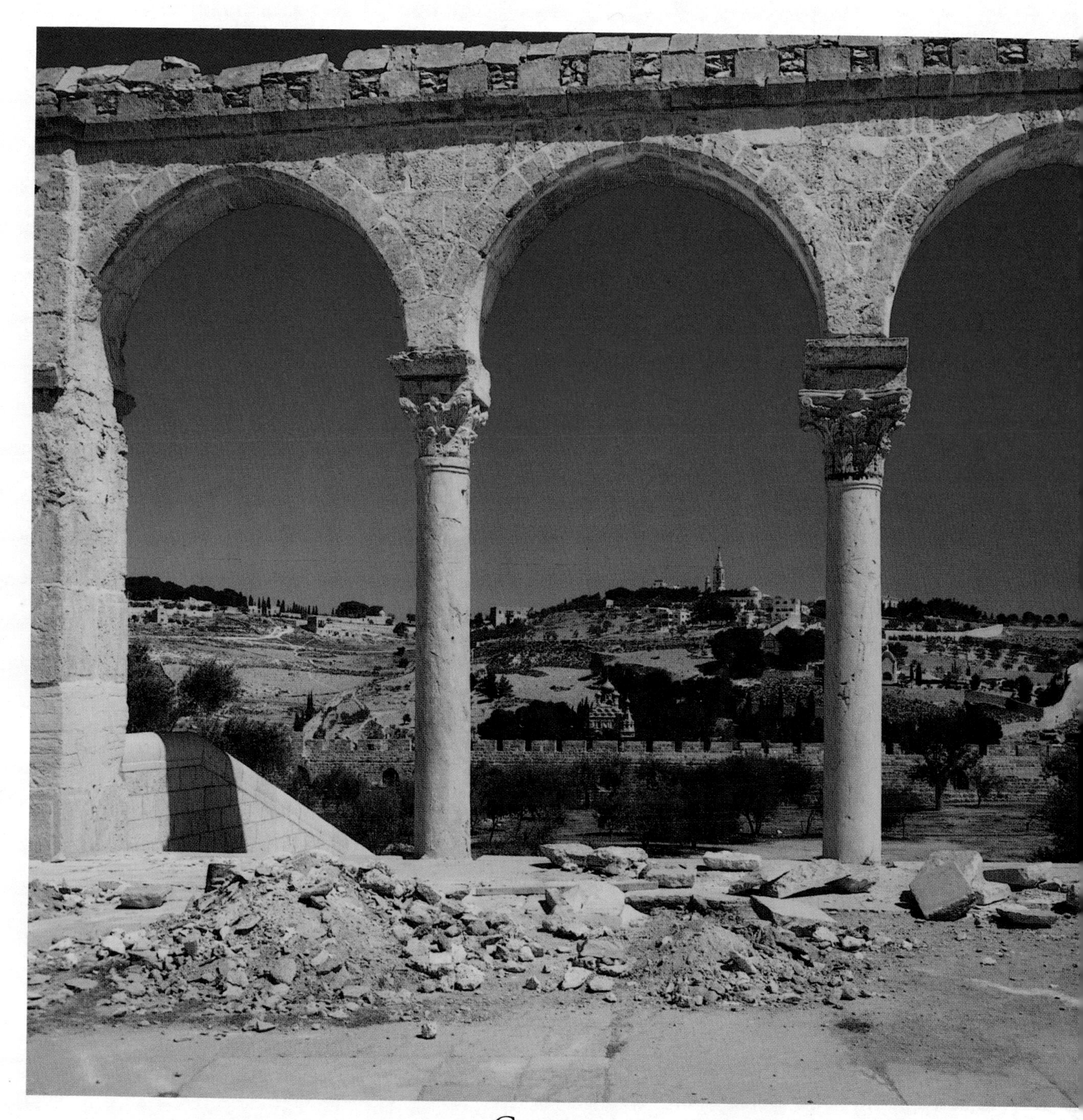

Generally believed to be the site of Jesus' ascension into heaven, the MOUNT OF ASCENSION is just north of Bethany. It is seen here from the site of Herod's and Solomon's temples in Jerusalem.

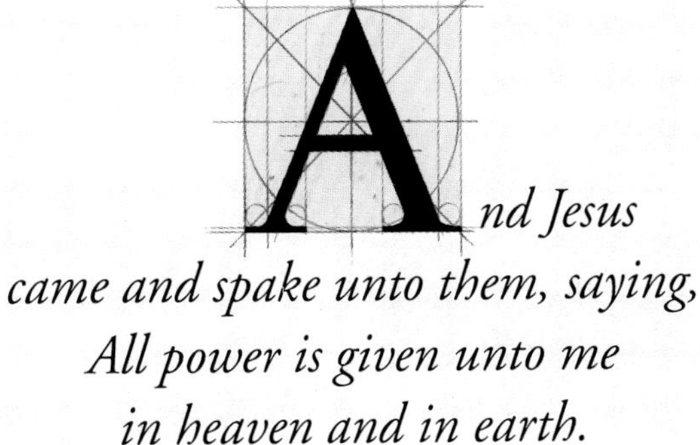

And Jesus
came and spake unto them, saying,
All power is given unto me
in heaven and in earth.

Go ye therefore, and teach all nations,
baptizing them in the name of the Father,
and of the Son, and of the Holy Ghost:
Teaching them to observe all things
whatsoever I have commanded you:
and, lo, I am with you alway,
even unto the end of the world.
Amen.

MATTHEW 28: 18-20

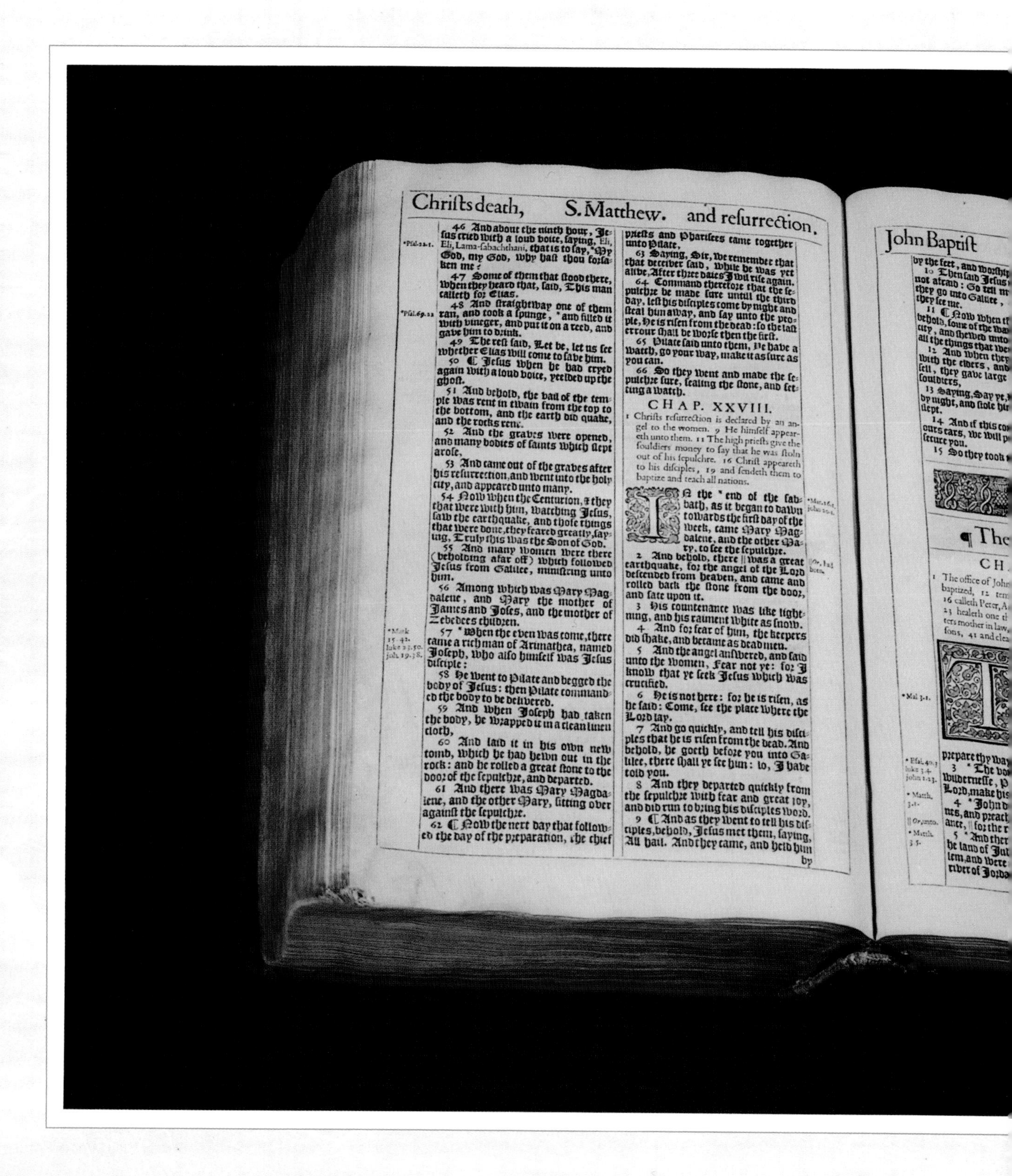

Christs death, S. Matthew. and resurrection.

46 And about the ninth houre, Jesus cried with a loud voice, saying, Eli, Eli, Lama-sabachthani, that is to say, *My God, my God, why hast thou forsaken me?

*Psal.22.1.

47 Some of them that stood there, when they heard that, said, This man calleth for Elias.

48 And straightway one of them ran, and tooke a spunge, *and filled it with vineger, and put it on a reed, and gave him to drinke.

*Psal.69.22

49 The rest said, Let be, let us see whether Elias will come to save him.

50 ¶ Jesus when he had cryed againe with a loud voice, yeelded up the ghost.

51 And behold, the vaile of the temple was rent in twaine from the top to the bottome, and the earth did quake, and the rocks rent.

52 And the graves were opened, and many bodies of saints which slept arose,

53 And came out of the graves after his resurrection, and went into the holy citie, and appeared unto many.

54 Now when the Centurion, & they that were with him, watching Jesus, saw the earthquake, and those things that were done, they feared greatly, saying, Truly this was the Sonne of God.

55 And many women were there (beholding afarre off) which followed Jesus from Galilee, ministring unto him.

56 Among which was Mary Magdalene, and Mary the mother of James and Joses, and the mother of Zebedees children.

57 *When the even was come, there came a rich man of Arimathea, named Joseph, who also himselfe was Jesus disciple:

*Mark 15.42. luke 23.50. joh.19.38.

58 He went to Pilate and begged the body of Jesus: then Pilate commanded the body to be delivered.

59 And when Joseph had taken the body, he wrapped it in a cleane linnen cloth,

60 And laid it in his owne new tombe, which he had hewen out in the rocke: and he rolled a great stone to the doore of the sepulchre, and departed.

61 And there was Mary Magdalene, and the other Mary, sitting over against the sepulchre.

62 ¶ Now the next day that followed the day of the preparation, the chiefe priests and Pharisees came together unto Pilate,

63 Saying, Sir, we remember that that deceiver said, while he was yet alive, After three daies I will rise againe.

64 Command therefore that the sepulchre be made sure untill the third day, lest his disciples come by night and steale him away, and say unto the people, He is risen from the dead: so the last errour shall be worse then the first.

65 Pilate said unto them, Ye have a watch, go your way, make it as sure as you can.

66 So they went and made the sepulchre sure, sealing the stone, and setting a watch.

CHAP. XXVIII.

1 Christs resurrection is declared by an angel to the women. 9 He himselfe appeareth unto them. 11 The high priests give the souldiers money to say that he was stoln out of his sepulchre. 16 Christ appeareth to his disciples, 19 and sendeth them to baptize and teach all nations.

In the *end of the sabbath, as it began to dawne towards the first day of the weeke, came Mary Magdalene, and the other Mary, to see the sepulchre.

*Mar.16.1. John 20.1.

2 And behold, there || was a great earthquake, for the angel of the Lord descended from heaven, and came and rolled backe the stone from the doore, and sate upon it.

|| Or, had been.

3 His countenance was like lightning, and his raiment white as snow.

4 And for feare of him, the keepers did shake, and became as dead men.

5 And the angel answered, and said unto the women, Feare not ye: for I know that ye seeke Jesus which was crucified.

6 He is not here: for he is risen, as he said: Come, see the place where the Lord lay.

7 And go quickly, and tell his disciples that he is risen from the dead. And behold, he goeth before you into Galilee, there shall ye see him: lo, I have told you.

8 And they departed quickly from the sepulchre with feare and great joy, and did run to bring his disciples word.

9 ¶ And as they went to tell his disciples, behold, Jesus met them, saying, All haile. And they came, and held him by

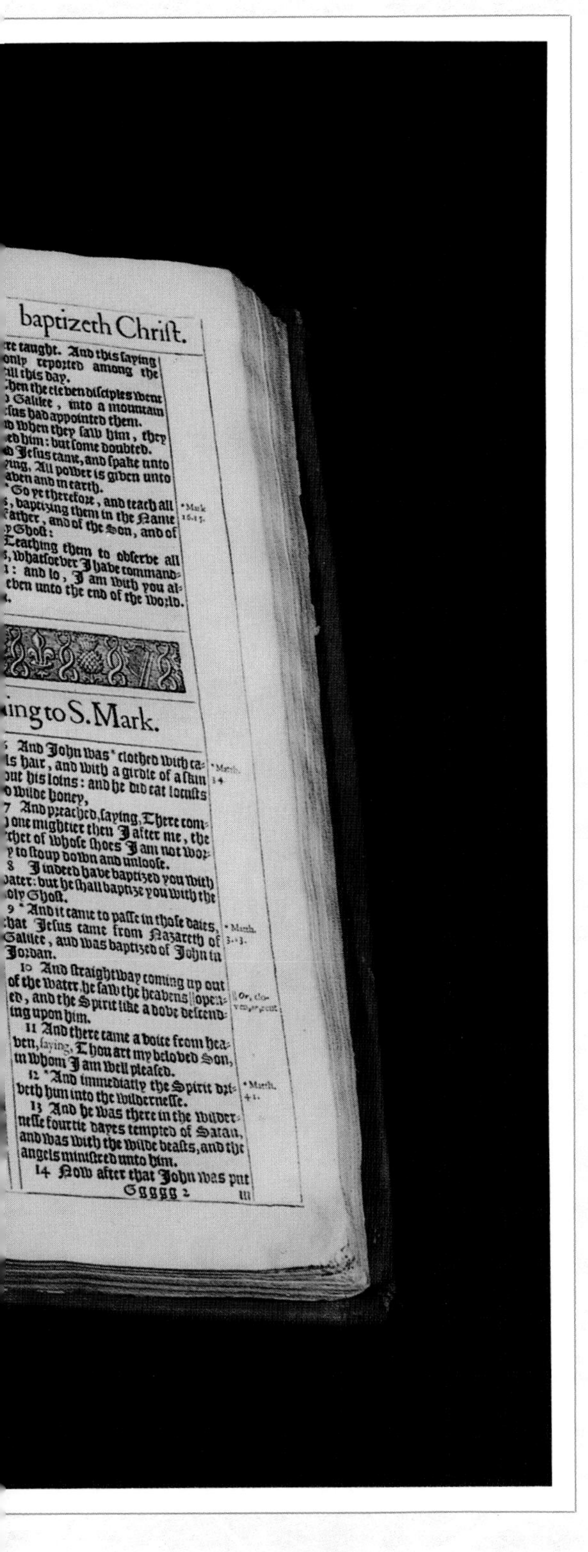

THE EARLY CHURCH

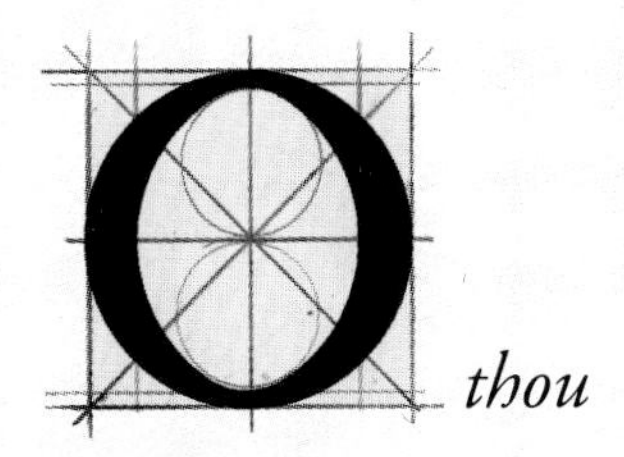

O thou

afflicted, tossed with tempest,

and not comforted, behold.

I will lay thy stones with fair colours,

and lay thy foundations with sapphires.

And all thy children shall be

taught of the LORD;

and great shall be the peace of thy children.

ISAIAH 54: 11, 13

Shortly after James I ascended to the throne of England in 1603, he convened a conference to settle many disputed matters with the Church of England, the most important being an authorized English translation of the Bible. For almost eight years a team of scholars worked on the translation, developing the beautiful and rhythmic prose we are familiar with today. Published in 1611, the KING JAMES VERSION of THE HOLY BIBLE quickly won acceptance from the English-speaking world. The Bible pictured dates from 1639. This edition was printed by Robert Barker, the same printer responsible for the 1611 first edition.

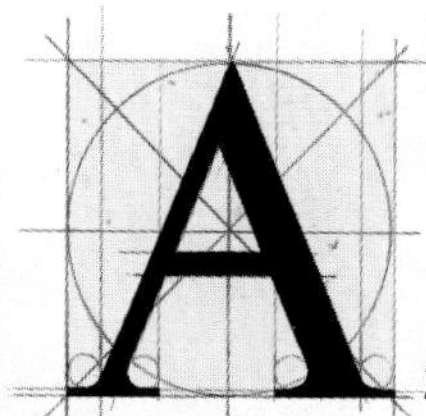

And when
the day of Pentecost was fully come,
they were all with one accord in one place.
And suddenly there came a sound
from heaven as of a rushing mighty wind,
and it filled all the house
where they were sitting.

And they were all filled
with the Holy Ghost,
and began to speak with other tongues,
as the Spirit gave them utterance.
And there were dwelling at Jerusalem
Jews, devout men, out of every nation
under heaven.
And they were all amazed,
and were in doubt, saying one to another,
What meaneth this?

ACTS 2: 1, 2, 4, 5, 12

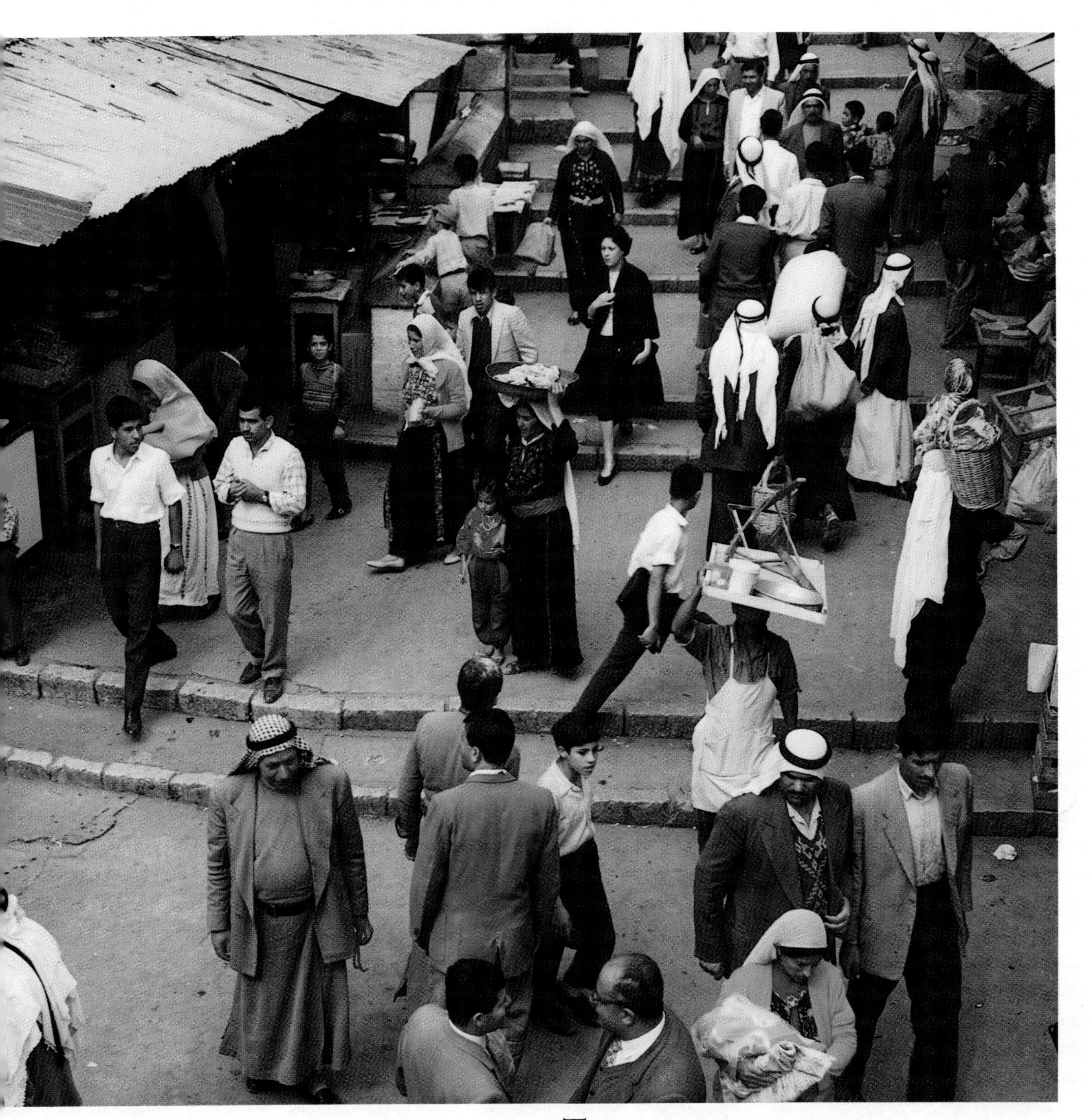

Today, as in Biblical times, the crowded streets of OLD JERUSALEM are filled with people of many different nations and beliefs.

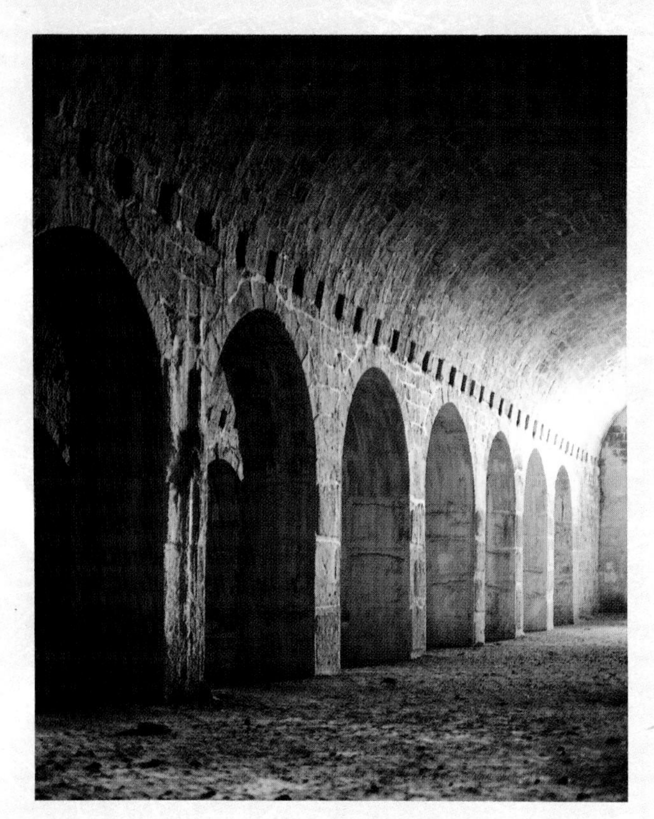

This site, believed to be SOLOMON'S STABLES, was unearthed near the Dome of the Rock. The once magnificent Temple of Solomon predated Herod's temple, which in turn gave way to the Moslem Dome of the Rock.

And by the hands of the apostles were many signs and wonders wrought among the people; (and they were all with one accord in Solomon's porch. And of the rest durst no man join himself to them: but the people magnified them. And believers were the more added to the Lord, multitudes both of men and women.)

There came also a multitude out of the cities round about unto Jerusalem, bringing sick folks, and them which were vexed with unclean spirits: and they were healed every one.

ACTS 5: 12-14, 16

There was a certain man in Caesarea called Cornelius. . . . A devout man . . . that . . . prayed to God alway. He saw in a vision . . . an angel of God coming in to him, and saying unto him. . . . send men to Joppa, and call for Simon, whose surname is Peter. . . .

Peter . . . said. . . . what is the cause wherefore ye are come? And they said, Cornelius . . . was warned from God by an holy angel to send for thee into his house. . . . And as Peter was coming in, Cornelius met him, and fell down at his feet, and worshipped him. But Peter took him up, saying, Stand up; I myself also am a man. Then Peter . . . said, of a truth I perceive that God is no respecter of persons: But in every nation he that feareth him, and worketh righteousness, is accepted with him. While Peter yet spake these words, the Holy Ghost fell on all them. . . . And he commanded them to be baptized in the name of the Lord.

ACTS 10: 1-5, 21, 22, 25, 26, 34, 35, 44, 48

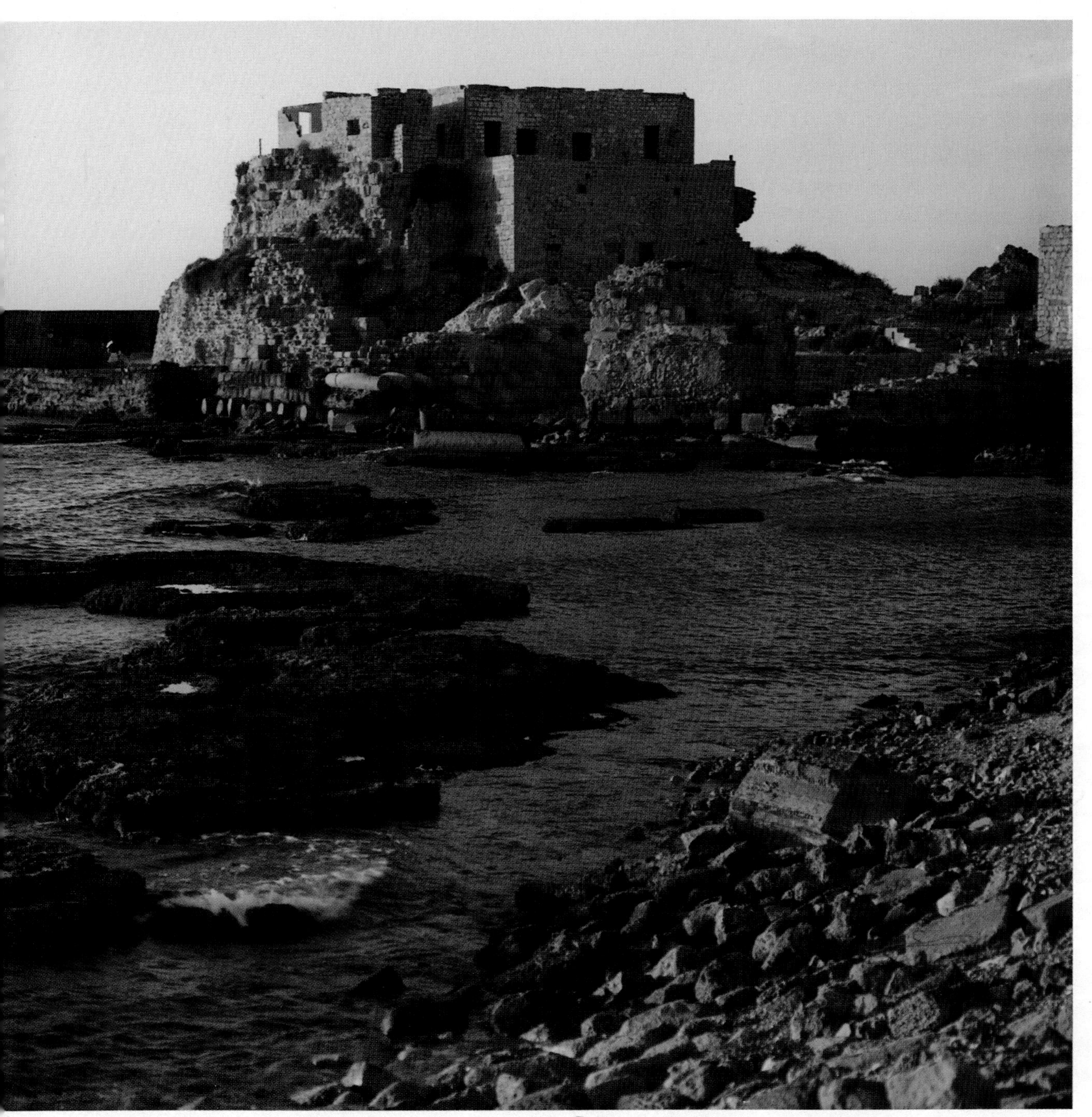

CAESAREA, a Roman city built by Herod, became an important Mediterranean seaport and was often visited by Paul.

Impressive ruins are all that remain of the ancient city of CORINTH, one of the most important and most corrupt cities in Greece. Despite the city's reputation, Paul was able to establish a church in Corinth by A.D. 51. The ruins pictured show the remains of the Temple of Apollo. Each fluted column (about 24 feet tall) was cut from a single block of stone from nearby quarries.

Though I speak with the tongues of men and of angels, and have not charity, I am become as sounding brass, or a tinkling cymbal. And though I have the gift of prophecy, and understand all mysteries, and all knowledge; and though I have all faith, so that I could remove mountains, and have not charity, I am nothing.

Charity suffereth long, and is kind; charity envieth not; charity vaunteth not itself, is not puffed up, Doth not behave itself unseemly, seeketh not her own, is not easily provoked, thinketh no evil; Beareth all things, believeth all things, hopeth all things, endureth all things.

When I was a child, I spake as a child, I understood as a child, I thought as a child: but when I became a man, I put away childish things. And now abideth faith, hope, charity, these three; but the greatest of these is charity.

1 CORINTHIANS 13: 1, 2, 4, 5, 7, 11, 13

*Now as touching
things offered unto idols, we know that we all
have knowledge. Knowledge puffeth up,
but charity edifieth. And if any man think that
he knoweth any thing, he knoweth nothing
yet as he ought to know.
But if any man love God, the
same is known of him.*

*As concerning therefore the eating of those
things that are offered in sacrifice unto idols,
we know that an idol is nothing in the world,
and that there is none other God but one.
For though there be that are called gods,
whether in heaven or in earth. . . .
But to us there is but one God, the Father,
of whom are all things, and we in him;
and one Lord Jesus Christ, by whom
are all things, and we by him.*

1 CORINTHIANS 8: 1-6

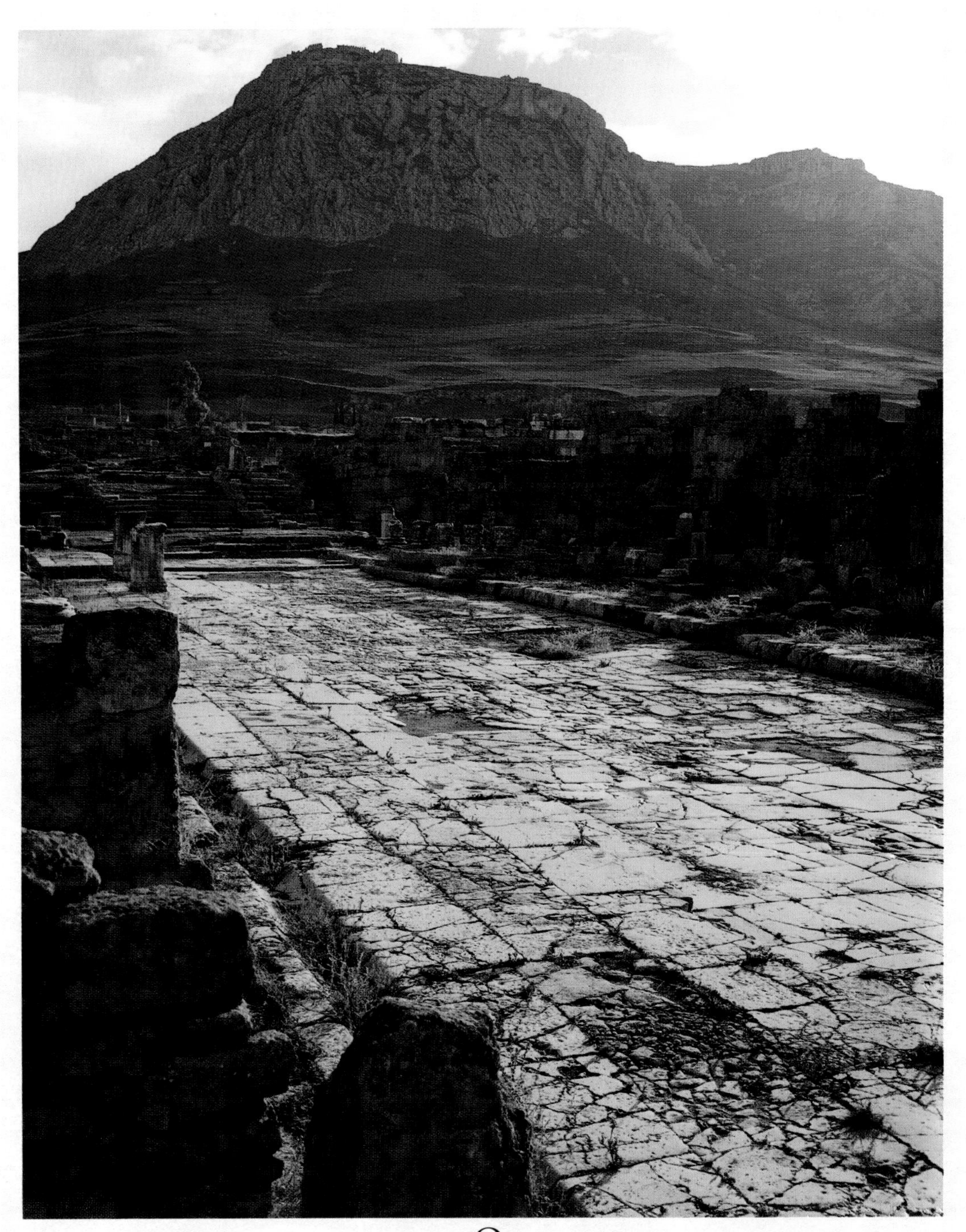

Once a prosperous and busy site, THE MARKETPLACE or *AGORA* in Corinth was paved with marble. Rebuilt many times during the centuries, Corinth was destroyed by earthquakes in A.D. 521 and again in 1858. Modern Corinth, a small town in comparison to its past, stands a few miles from the ancient site.

MARS' HILL, located between the Acropolis and the *Agora* in Athens, was a busy area. The Parthenon, visible on top of the Acropolis was built in 500 B.C. as a temple to Athena, the Greek goddess of wisdom and war, and was already an ancient landmark when Paul visited the city on his travels.

Then Paul
stood in the midst of Mars' hill,
and said, Ye men of Athens,
I perceive that in all things ye are too
superstitious. For as I passed by . . .
I found an altar with this inscription,
TO THE UNKNOWN GOD.
Whom therefore ye ignorantly worship,
him declare I unto you.
God that made the world
and all things therein, seeing
that he is Lord of heaven and earth,
dwelleth not in temples made with hands;
Neither is worshipped with men's hands,
as though he needed any thing,
seeing he giveth to all life, and breath,
and all things. . . .
For in him we live, and move,
and have our being. . . .

ACTS 17: 22-25, 28

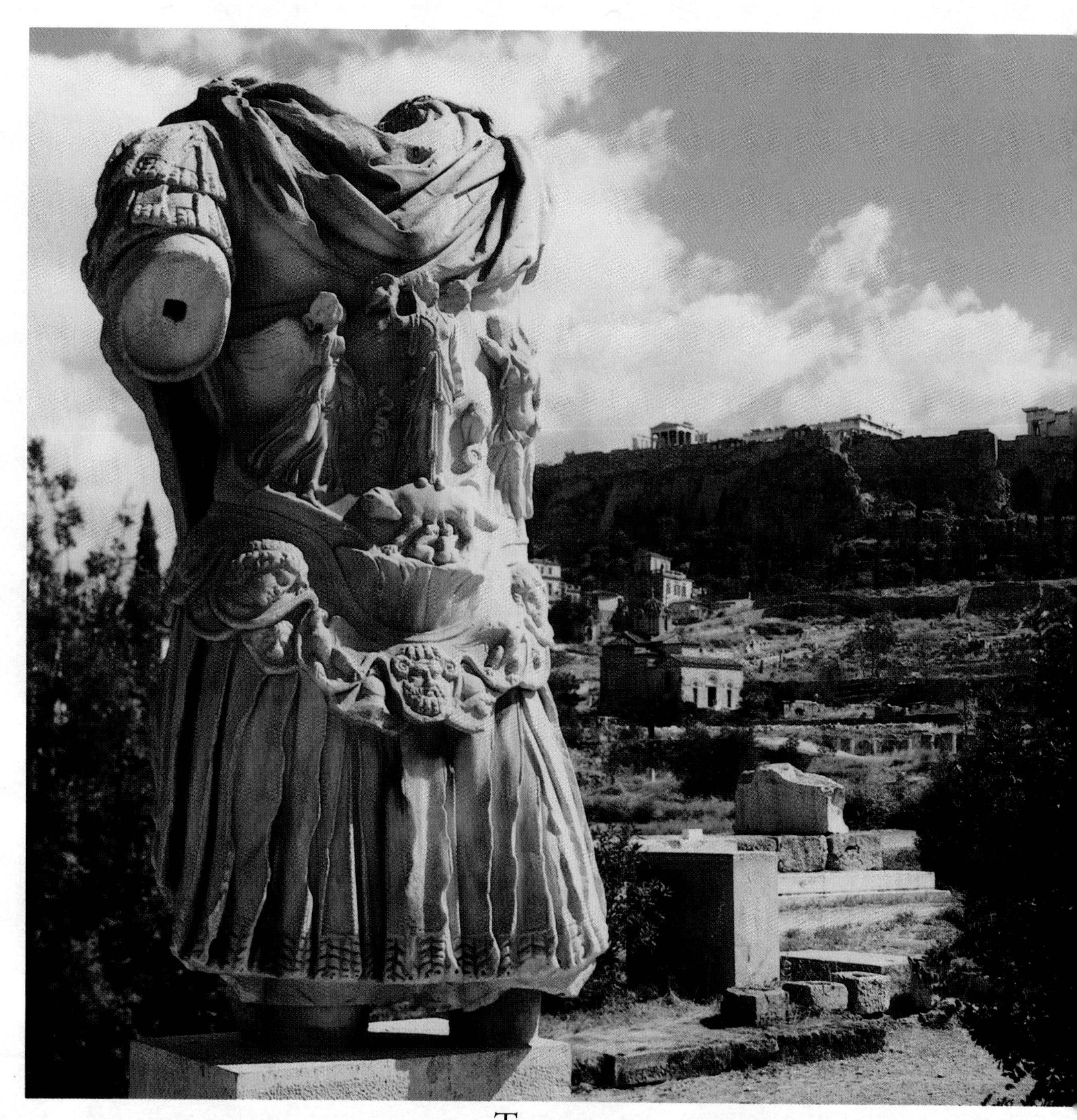

The Athens of New Testament time was an independent city filled with learned scholars and debaters, many of whom gathered in the *AGORA.* The statue is of the Roman Emperor Hadrian, an admired administrator, builder, and soldier. His plans to build a new city at Jerusalem to honor the god Jupiter touched off a revolt in the years A.D. 132 to 135 which was brutally repressed by Rome.

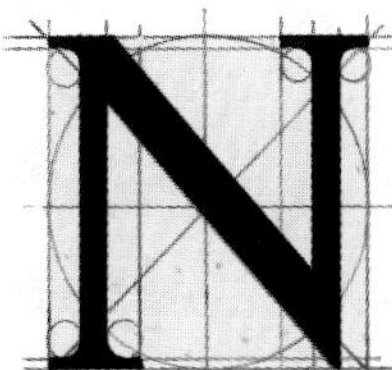

Now while
Paul waited for them at Athens, his spirit
was stirred in him, when he saw the city
wholly given to idolatry.
Therefore disputed he in the synagogue
with the Jews, and with the devout
persons, and in the market daily
with them that met with him.

Then certain philosophers of the Epicureans,
and of the Stoicks, encountered him.
And some said, What will this babbler say?
other some, He seemeth to be
a setter forth of strange gods:
because he preached unto them
Jesus, and the resurrection.

ACTS 17: 16-18

And there sat a certain man at Lystra. . . . being a cripple from his mother's womb, who never had walked: The same heard Paul speak: who steadfastly beholding him, and perceiving that he had faith to be healed, Said with a loud voice, Stand upright on thy feet. And he leaped and walked. And when the people saw what Paul had done, they lifted up their voices, saying . . . The gods are come down to us in the likeness of men.

And they called Barnabas, Jupiter; and Paul, Mercurius, because he was the chief speaker.

ACTS 14: 8-12

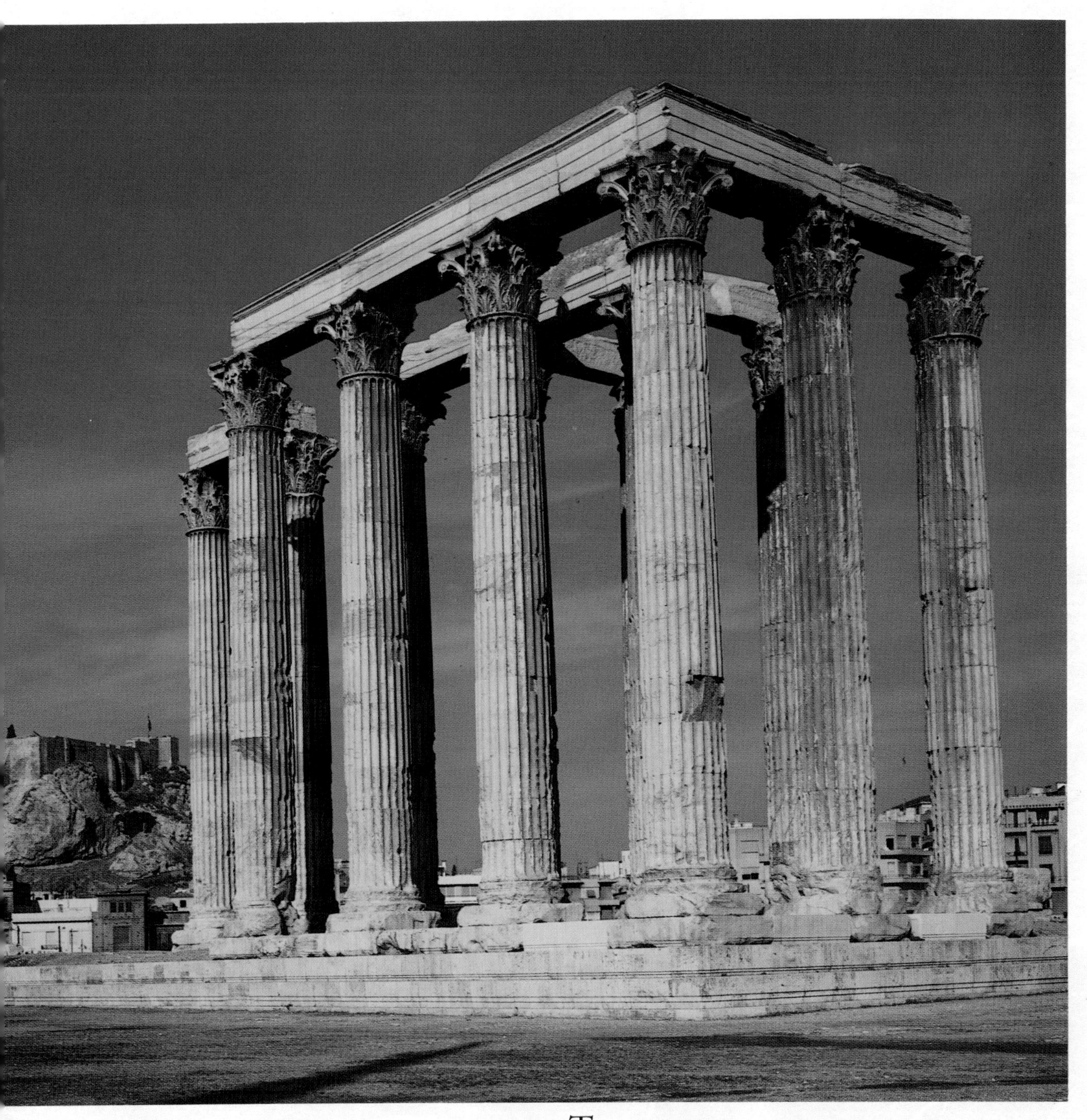

The massive ruins of the TEMPLE OF ZEUS still stand below the Acropolis in Athens. Zeus, whom the Romans called Jupiter, was the supreme god in Greek mythology and considered to be the father of other gods and many mortal heroes.

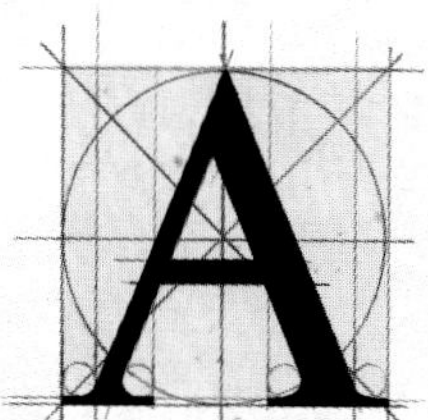

nd the same
time there arose no small stir about that way.
For a certain man named Demetrius,
a silversmith which made silver shrines for
Diana, brought no small gain unto the
craftsmen; Whom he called together . . .
and said, Sirs, ye know that by
this craft we have our wealth.
Moreover ye see and hear, that . . . almost
throughout all Asia, this Paul hath persuaded
and turned away much people, saying that they
be no gods, which are made with hands:
So that not only this our craft is in danger . . .
but also that the temple of the great goddess
Diana should be despised, and her
magnificence should be destroyed, whom all
Asia and the world worshippeth.

And when they heard these sayings,
they were full of wrath, and cried out, saying,
Great is Diana of the Ephesians. And
the whole city was filled with confusion. . . .

ACTS 19: 23-29

Ephesus, at one time the largest city on the west coast of Asia Minor, was a cosmopolitan city filled with a diverse population open to new ideas. This THEATER, which seated 25,000, was where the silversmith Demetrius gathered his co-workers to discuss Paul's condemnation of the goddess Diana.

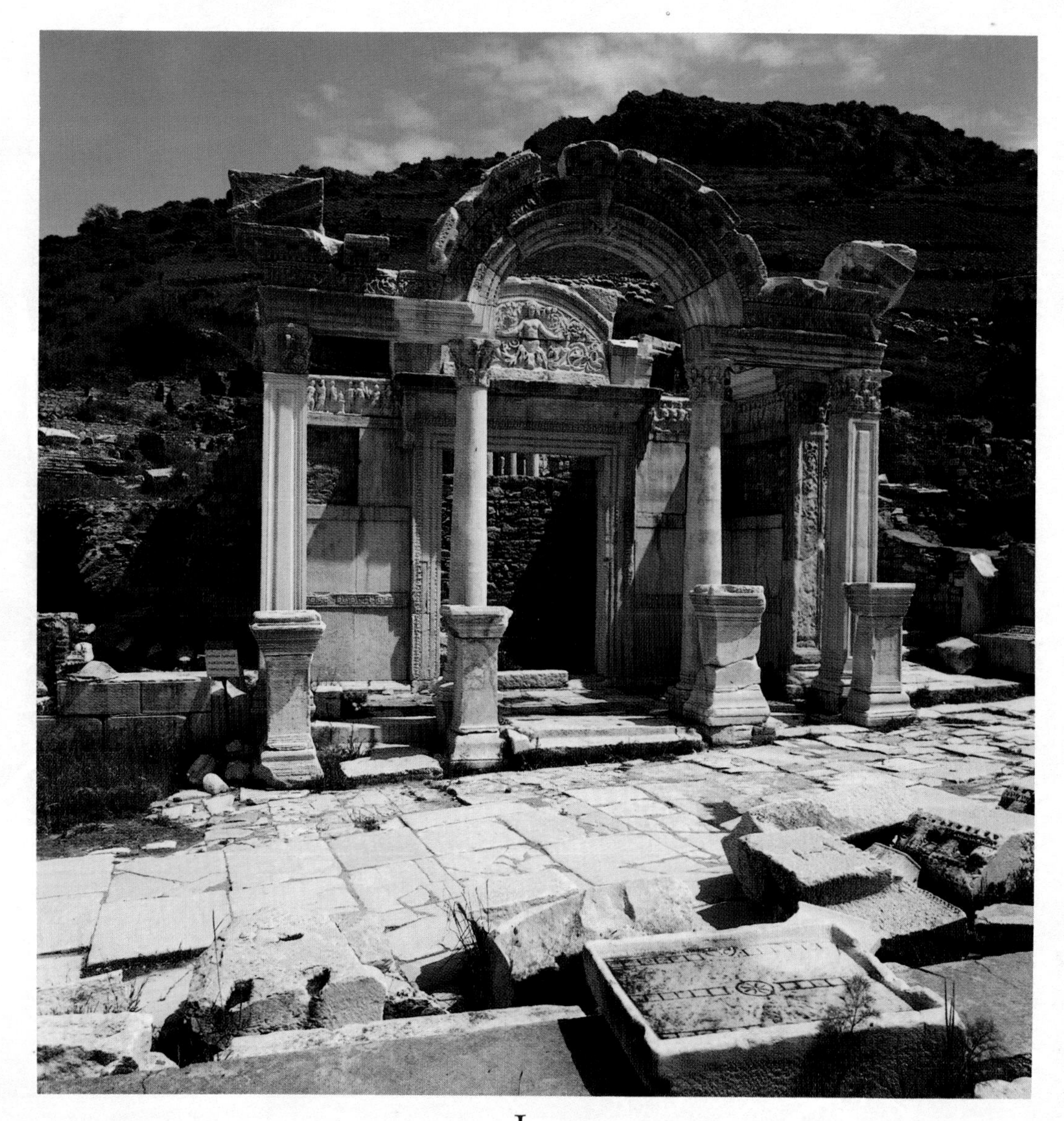

Little remains today of the ancient city of EPHESUS, located on the western coast of Turkey. The once magnificent Temple of Diana, the Roman goddess of the hunt and the moon, has been reduced to just a few broken pieces of column. The temple ruins pictured here were once part of a towering structure built to honor the Roman Emperor Hadrian.

I therefore, the
prisoner of the Lord, beseech you that ye
walk worthy of the vocation
wherewith ye are called,
With all lowliness and meekness,
with longsuffering,
forebearing one another in love;
Endeavouring to keep the unity
of the Spirit in the bond of peace.

There is one body, and one Spirit,
even as ye are called
in one hope of your calling;
One Lord, one faith, one baptism,
One God and Father of all,
who is above all, and through all,
and in you all.
But unto every one of us
is given grace according to the measure
of the gift of Christ.

EPHESIANS 4: 1-7

Christians turned out all along the APPIAN WAY (which at one time covered over 350 miles) to welcome Paul on his journey into Rome, meeting him first about 40 miles south of the city at the Forum of Appius and then at Three Taverns, a well-known way station.

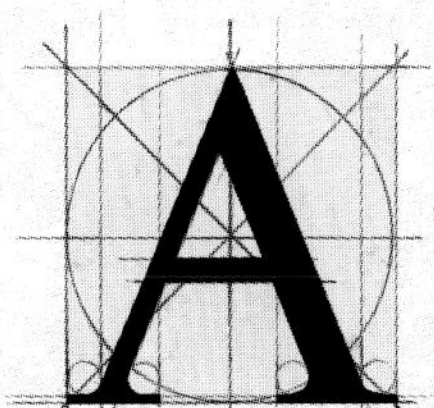*nd so we went toward Rome. And from thence, when the brethren heard of us, they came to meet us as far as Appiiforum, and The three taverns: whom when Paul saw, he thanked God, and took courage.*

And when we came to Rome, the centurion delivered the prisoners to the captain of the guard: but Paul was suffered to dwell by himself with a soldier that kept him.

And Paul dwelt two whole years in his own hired house, and received all that came in unto him, Preaching the kingdom of God, and teaching those things which concern the Lord Jesus Christ, with all confidence, no man forbidding him.

ACTS 28: 14-16, 30-31

Therefore being
justified by faith, we have peace with
God through our Lord Jesus Christ:
By whom also we have access by faith
into this grace wherein we stand,
and rejoice in hope of
the glory of God. And not only so,
but we glory in tribulations also:
knowing that tribulation
worketh patience;
And patience, experience;
and experience, hope:
And hope maketh not ashamed;
because the love of God is shed
abroad in our hearts
by the Holy Ghost
which is given unto us.

ROMANS 5: 1-5

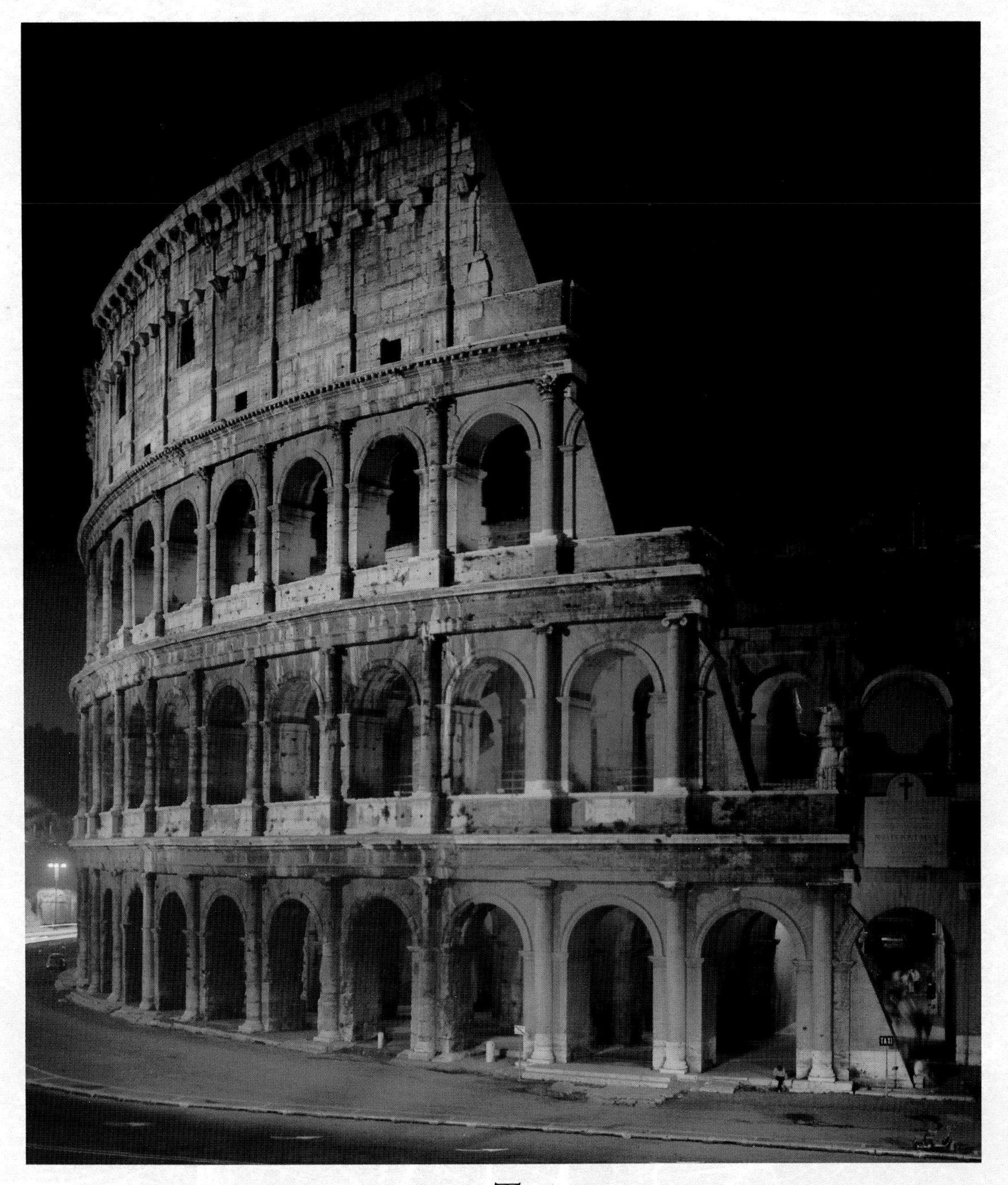

The ROMAN COLOSSEUM was completed in A.D. 80 by the Emperor Titus. Over the next few centuries it was the scene of the deaths of thousands of Christians forced into deadly games for the amusement of the crowds of up to 45,000 spectators.

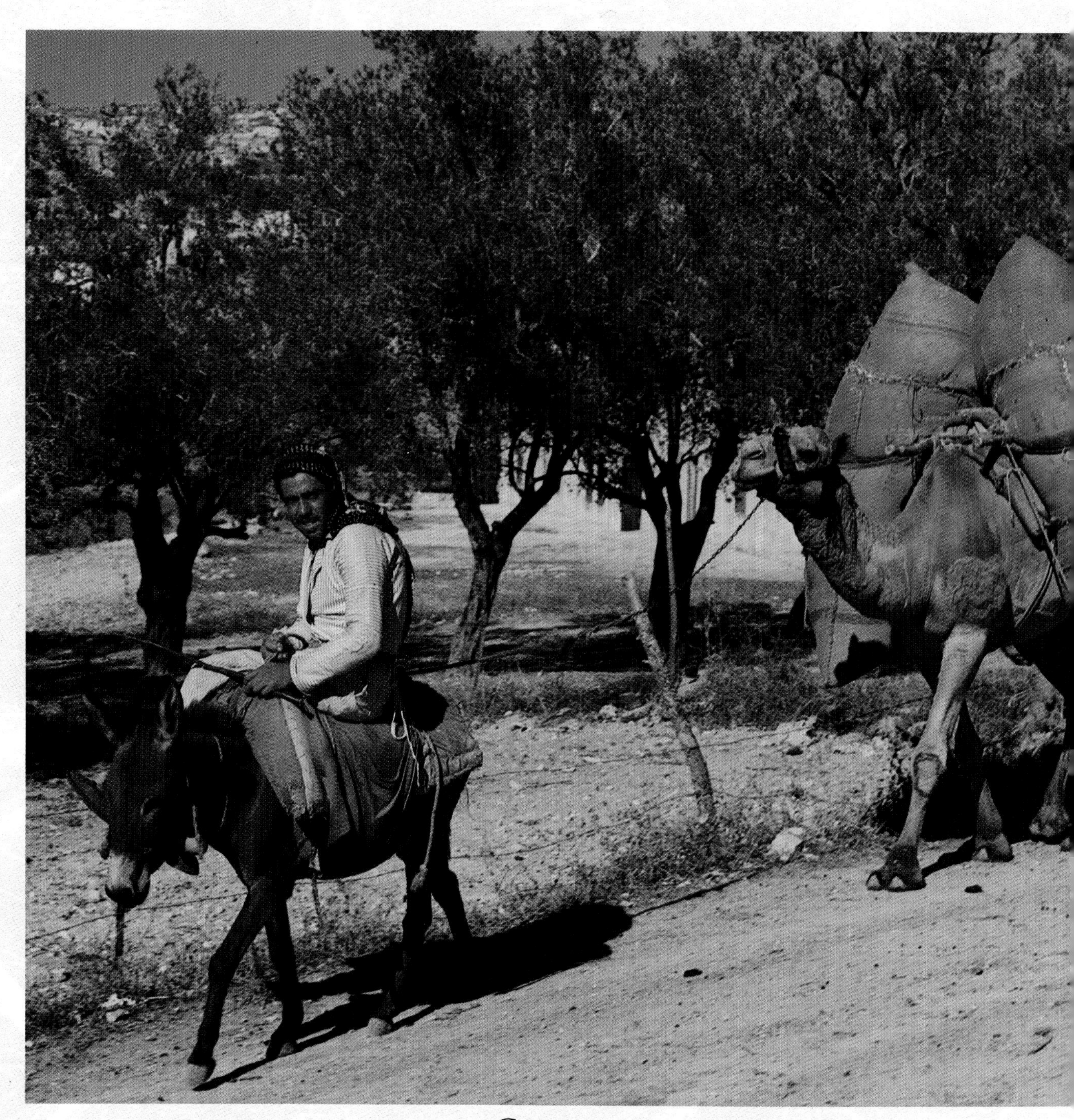

CAMELS are still used as beasts of burden in the Holy Land. Here a man leads a heavily laden camel caravan past a grove of young olive trees on the road near Nazareth.

Doth a fountain send forth at the same place sweet water and bitter? Can the fig tree, my brethren, bear olive berries? either a vine, figs? so can no fountain both yield salt water and fresh.

Who is a wise man and endued with knowledge among you? let him shew out of a good conversation his works with meekness of wisdom.

But if ye have bitter envying and strife in your hearts, glory not, and lie not against the truth. For where envying and strife is, there is confusion and every evil work.

But the wisdom that is from above is first pure, then peaceable, gentle, and easy to be intreated, full of mercy and good fruits, without partiality, and without hypocrisy. And the fruit of righteousness is sown in peace of them that make peace.

JAMES 3: 11-14, 16-18

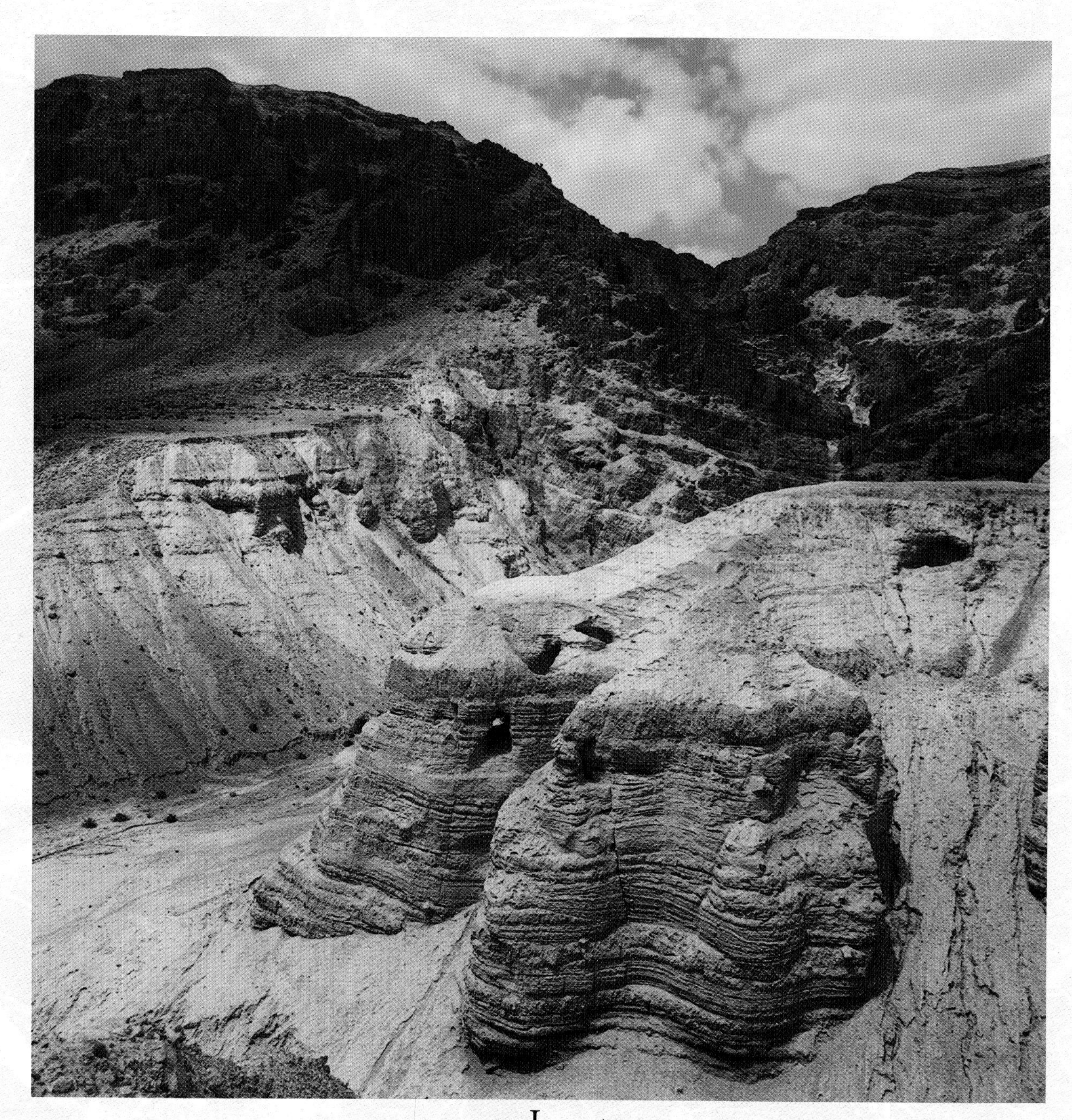

In 1947, ancient writings that became known as the DEAD SEA SCROLLS were found in caves near present-day Khirbet Qumran on the northwestern shore of the Dead Sea. Scholars are still translating these ancient manuscripts, which were written between 250 B.C. and A.D. 68.

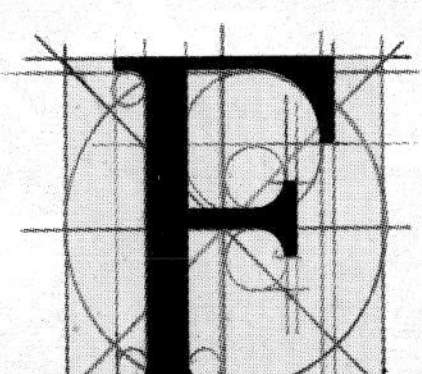

or God so loved the world, that he gave his only begotten Son, that whosoever believeth in him should not perish, but have everlasting life. For God sent not his Son into the world to condemn the world; but that the world through him might be saved.

JOHN 3: 16-17

BIOGRAPHIES, MAPS, AND PHOTOGRAPHY INDEX

THIS SMALL VILLAGE is typical of many throughout the Holy Land. It was from such ordinary and unpretentious surroundings that Jesus called his disciples.

The First Twelve Disciples

Jesus, early in His ministry, chose twelve men to be His disciples — His students. Each man was chosen from fishermen, from tax collectors, and from unknown, but most certainly undistinguished, careers. We know little of the personal life of these first twelve. From the biblical account alone, these men appeared to be, for the most part, uneducated and, to us looking back, incredibly slow to grasp the fact that they were witnessing events which would forever change the future of mankind. In short, these first disciples were ordinary men of ordinary intelligence, but who, through the grace of God, left an extraordinary legacy for the world.

Peter

A fisherman from the shores of the Sea of Galilee and an early follower of John the Baptist, Peter is first among the apostles in many ways. He was the first disciple called by Jesus, the first to recognize Jesus as Lord, and the first to recognize Jesus after His resurrection. Originally called Simon, he received the name Peter, "the rock," from Jesus. Peter is the only disciple known to have been married. A brother to Andrew, Peter was the most frequent spokesman of the apostles traveling to Antioch and Rome healing the sick. He is believed to have been crucified upside down in Rome.

Andrew

Also a follower of John the Baptist, it was Andrew who introduced his brother Peter to Jesus. One of the inner circle of disciples, Andrew was present during most of Jesus' ministry. He is the one who brought Jesus' attention to the boy with the two fishes and five loaves at the miraculous feeding of the 5,000 people. He is known to have preached around the Black Sea in Cappadocia, Russia, Byzantium, and Macedonia and is believed to have been martyred in Greece by crucifixion on an X-shaped cross.

Simon

Often referred to as Simon the Zealot, Simon possessed a zeal for Jewish law and rights. He preached along the shores of the Black Sea, as well as in Egypt and North Africa. He is reputed to have died in Iberia, but there is no record of his burial place.

Philip

A native of Bethsaida in Galilee, Philip is seen as shy, naive, and sober-minded. He was present at the miracle of the loaves and fishes; and when asked how they could feed the 5,000 people, Philip began calculating the amount of food they would need and its cost. Philip's ministry took him to Scythia, and he eventually died in Hieropolis.

Bartholomew

Not much is known about Bartholomew, who was introduced to Christ by Philip. Some scholars believe that the Bartholomew named in Matthew, Mark, and Luke may be the same person referred to as Nathaniel in the Book of John. According to tradition, Bartholomew traveled widely, preaching the gospel with Philip and Thomas throughout India, Mesopotamia, and Parthia. It is believed that he was crucified.

THE FIRST TWELVE DISCIPLES

MATTHEW

Before his decision to follow Christ, Matthew was by trade a tax collector, an occupation considered on a level with harlots, murderers, and robbers. Originally known as Levi, Matthew is not specifically mentioned again in the New Testament after he was called to be a disciple. It was traditionally believed that he was the author of the Book of Matthew; however, Matthew is known to have written in Aramaic and the Book of Matthew was originally composed in Greek. Some scholars now surmise that the Book of Matthew was written anonymously by a Palestinian Jew who drew heavily on the Gospels of Mark and a Greek translation of Matthew's earlier writings.

JOHN

The disciple described as the most beloved of Jesus, John is the one to whom the crucified Jesus entrusted the care of His mother. John is believed to have been the son of Salome, who may have been a sister to Jesus' mother. John's ministry took him through Asia Minor and eventually forced him into exile in Patmos. It is generally believed that John is the author of the Book of John. His authorship of Revelation, which was long believed, is now disputed. According to some writings, John lived to a very old age and is reputed to be buried in Ephesus.

JAMES THE LESS

The son of one of the Marys who went to Jesus' tomb on the morning of the third day, James the Less became an apostle during the second year of Jesus' ministry. His designation as "the less" could mean that he was the lesser known of the two disciples named James, or it could refer to a small stature. His original Greek name, "*Mikros,*" means either small or less.

THOMAS

Thomas was the first disciple to recognize Christ's divinity, but he will forever be remembered as "doubting Thomas" because of his refusal to acknowledge Christ's resurrection until he saw Jesus' wounds. Although tradition places him as far a field as India, Thomas is known to have spread the gospel in Parthia and Persia, where he is said to have died.

JAMES

The older brother of John, James was the first disciple to suffer martyrdom. He and his brother may have been strong-minded individuals, since they were often called "sons of thunder" by Jesus. James became the first apostle to Spain. He was killed on the order of Herod Agrippa I, the grandson of Herod the Great.

JUDE

Some scholars believe that Jude was the younger brother of Jesus and that he is the author of the Epistle of Jude. His missionary work took him throughout Palestine, Syria, and Mesopotamia, and eventually led to his probable martyrdom in Persia.

JUDAS ISCARIOT

The only one of the twelve disciples not from Galilee, Judas, a Judean, is the man who turned traitor to Jesus in exchange for thirty pieces of silver. Judas was the treasurer for the disciples and therefore had access to money, so it is not known why he accepted a relatively small amount to betray Jesus. Some scholars speculate that Judas hoped it would force Jesus into using His power against the Romans; others say that Judas may have become convinced that Jesus was a false Messiah; still others say that he was disturbed over Jesus' association with sinners. Later, with great remorse for what he had done, Judas is said in the Book of Matthew to have hanged himself. According to Acts, however, he bought a burial field with his blood money, collapsed, and died there.

Two Who Chose to Follow the Risen Christ

After His resurrection, Jesus called two more men who became so instrumental in the spreading of His Gospel, that they are included in this discussion of the Disciples. These two well-educated men, Paul and Luke, are responsible for the bulk of the New Testament and their writings helped ensure that the Word would, not only spread, but continue forever.

Paul

Even though he enjoyed the privilege of being born a Roman citizen, Paul and his family did not deny their Jewish heritage. It was Paul's zeal for the Jewish faith that led him on a campaign to suppress the followers of Jesus. At the height of this crusade, Paul was confronted by Jesus on the road to Damascus and in an instant Paul's life was changed. He became one of the most ardent supporters of Christ and is responsible for spreading the gospel to the Gentiles. Paul's travels and writings are well documented; he is considered one of the most important interpreters of Christ's message. Paul's letters to the Romans, Corinthians, Galatians, Ephesians, Philippians, Colossians, and Thessalonians, along with his Epistles to Philemon, Titus, and Timothy, comprise a large percentage of the New Testament. He is believed to have been executed in Rome, on the order of the Emperor Nero.

Luke

A Gentile, originally from Antioch, Luke is believed to be the author of the Gospel of Luke and the Acts of the Apostles. The only non-Jewish author of the New Testament, he was a close associate of Paul and traveled with him on most of his journeys. During Paul's imprisonment in Caesarea, Luke remained nearby and is thought to have used this time to gather oral and written material which he used in composing his record of the Gospels. Even though a quarter of the New Testament is attributed to Luke, he never mentions himself by name. Luke was a well-educated, careful historian and was known for his concern for the poor, sick, and outcast. He was called "the beloved physician" by Paul.

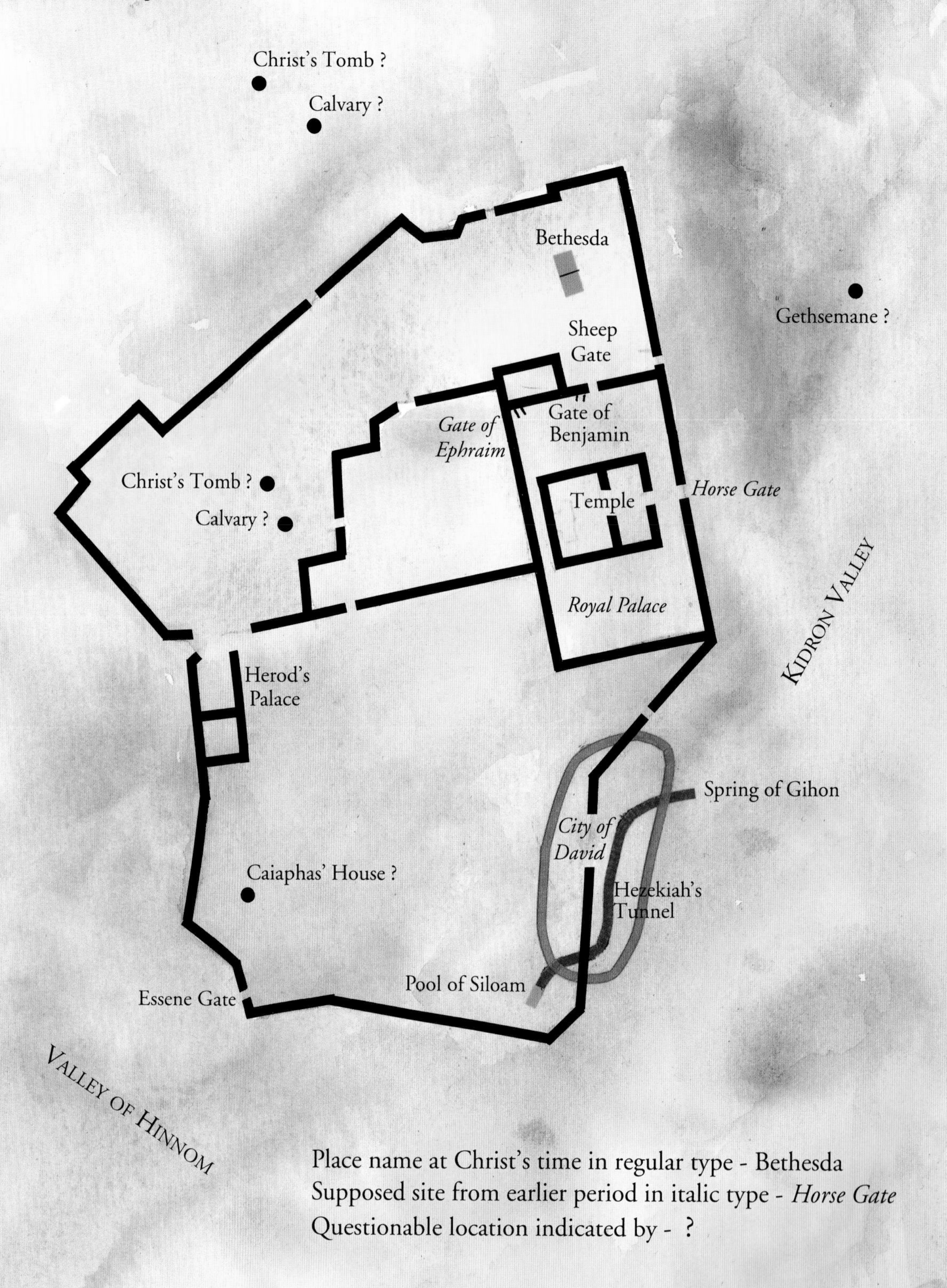
CHRIST'S JERUSALEM
Christ's Tomb ?
Calvary ?
Bethesda
Gethsemane ?
Sheep Gate
Gate of Ephraim
Gate of Benjamin
Christ's Tomb ?
Calvary ?
Temple
Horse Gate
Kidron Valley
Royal Palace
Herod's Palace
Spring of Gihon
City of David
Caiaphas' House ?
Hezekiah's Tunnel
Pool of Siloam
Essene Gate
Valley of Hinnom
Place name at Christ's time in regular type - Bethesda
Supposed site from earlier period in italic type - Horse Gate
Questionable location indicated by - ?

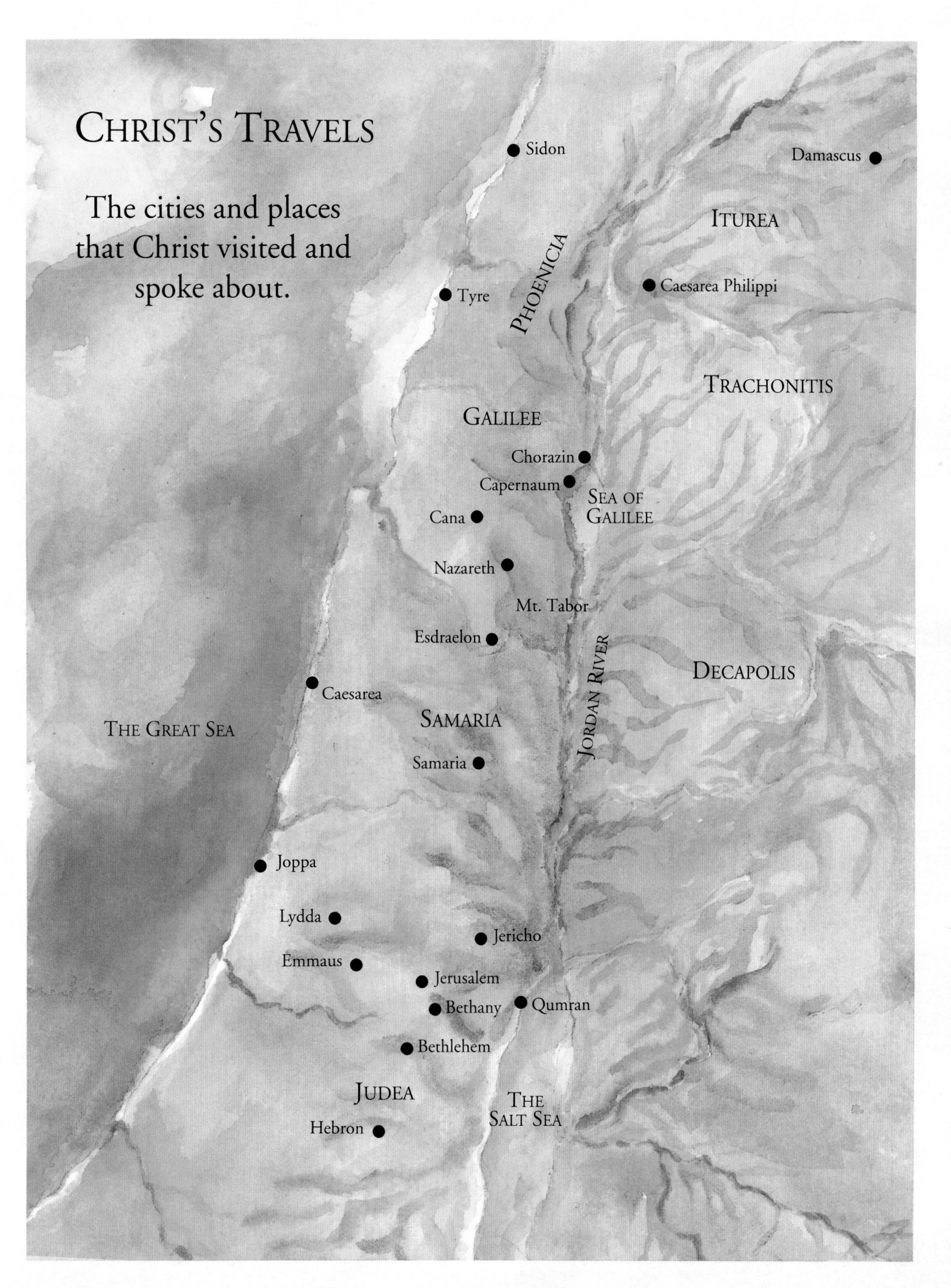
Christ's Travels
The cities and places that Christ visited and spoke about.
Sidon
Damascus
Iturea
Phoenicia
Tyre
Caesarea Philippi
Trachonitis
Galilee
Chorazin
Capernaum
Sea of Galilee
Cana
Nazareth
Mt. Tabor
Esdraelon
Jordan River
Decapolis
Caesarea
Samaria
The Great Sea
Samaria
Joppa
Lydda
Jericho
Emmaus
Jerusalem
Bethany
Qumran
Bethlehem
Judea
The Salt Sea
Hebron

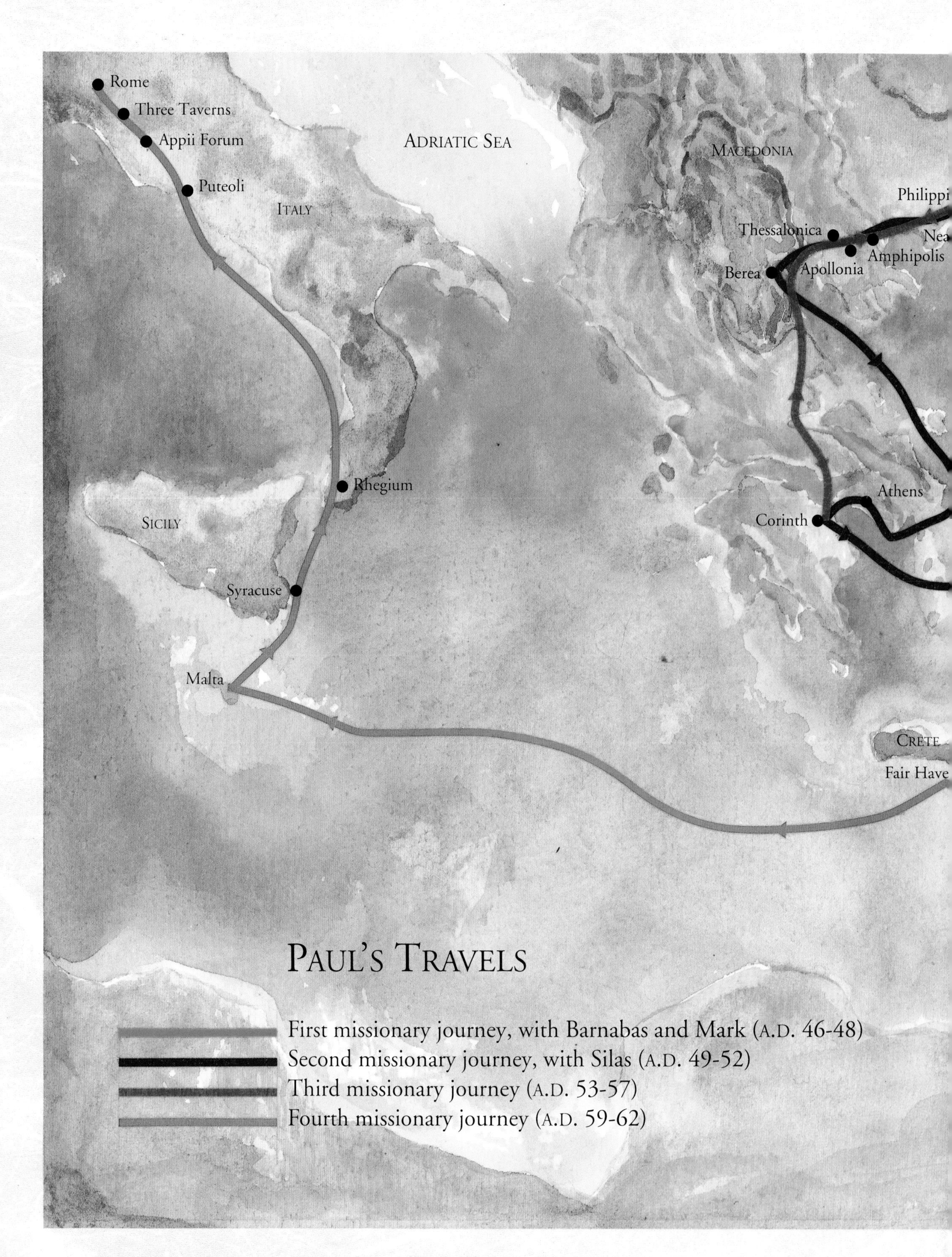
Rome
Three Taverns
Appii Forum
Puteoli
Italy
Adriatic Sea
Macedonia
Philippi
Thessalonica
Nea
Amphipolis
Berea
Apollonia
Rhegium
Sicily
Syracuse
Athens
Corinth
Malta
Crete
Fair Have
Paul's Travels
First missionary journey, with Barnabas and Mark (A.D. 46-48)
Second missionary journey, with Silas (A.D. 49-52)
Third missionary journey (A.D. 53-57)
Fourth missionary journey (A.D. 59-62)

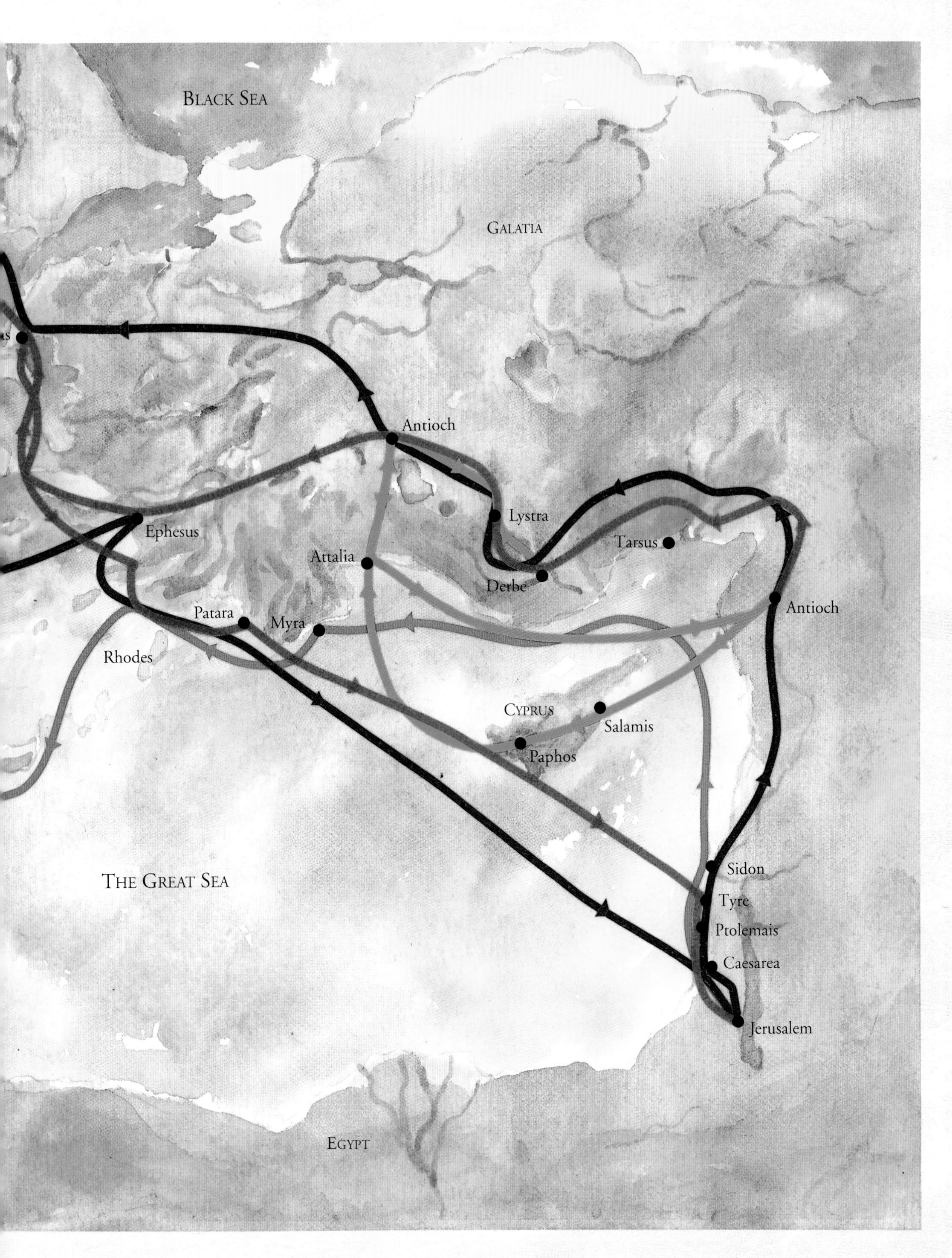
BLACK SEA
GALATIA
Antioch
Lystra
Tarsus
Ephesus
Attalia
Derbe
Antioch
Patara
Myra
Rhodes
CYPRUS
Salamis
Paphos
Sidon
THE GREAT SEA
Tyre
Ptolemais
Caesarea
Jerusalem
EGYPT

Photography Index

Photo Source for historic Bibles on pages 5, 35, 55, 69, 83, 111 - SuperStock, Inc.

ABOUT THE PHOTOGRAPHER: Russ Busby was born in Missouri and has had the privilege of traveling to over fifty countries on six continents as a photographer for the Billy Graham Evangelistic Association. Mr. Busby currently resides in California and says, "My desire is to open your eyes and heart—through pictures—to the unlimited possibilities God has waiting for each of us, when we truly seek Him."

SPECIAL OFFER: Ideals Publishing Corporation offers a clear acrylic reading stand for only $7.95 to protect and feature your copy of IN THE FOOTSTEPS OF THE MASTER. Order product # ID 10716, make your check payable to Ideals Publishing Corporation, and send the order information with your name and mailing address to: Catalog Department, Ideals Publishing Corporation, P.O. Box 14800, Nashville, TN 37214-8000

A
B
C
D
E
F
G
H
I
J